The End of Time?

The End of Time?

The Provocation of Talking about God

Proceedings of a meeting of Joseph Cardinal Ratzinger,
Johann Baptist Metz, Jürgen Moltmann,
and Eveline Goodman-Thau in Ahaus

Edited by Tiemo Rainer Peters and Claus Urban

English edition translated and edited by J. Matthew Ashley

Paulist Press
New York/Mahwah, N.J.

Book and cover design by Lynn Else

Title of the original edition: *Ende der Zeit?* Copyright © 1999 by Matthias-Grünewald-Verlag, Mainz, Germany

English translation copyright © 2004 by Paulist Press, Inc.

Library of Congress Cataloging-in-Publication Data

Ende der Zeit. English.
    The end of time? : the provocation of talking about God : proceedings of a meeting of Joseph Cardinal Ratzinger, Johann Baptist Metz, Jürgen Moltmann, and Eveline Goodman-Thau in Ahaus / edited by Tiemo Rainer Peters and Claus Urban ; translated and edited by J. Matthew Ashley.
        p. cm.
    ISBN 0-8091-4170-1 (alk paper)
    1. God—Congresses. 2. Eschatology—Congresses. 3. Time—Religious aspects—Christianity—Congresses. I. Peters, Tiemo Rainer, 1938– II. Urban, Claus, 1943– III. Ashley, James Matthew, 1958– IV. Title.

BT103.E53 2004
230—dc22

                                                                    2004013311

Published by Paulist Press
997 Macarthur Boulevard
Mahwah, New Jersey 07430

www.paulistpress.com

Printed and bound in the
United States of America

Contents

Translator's Introduction

North American readers may find it helpful to know a little of the history that lies behind this symposium, particularly concerning the relationship of its two primary participants, Professor Johann Baptist Metz and Cardinal Joseph Ratzinger.[1] In 1979 Metz headed the list to replace Heinrich Fries in the chair of dogmatic theology at the University of Munich. After becoming prominent as one of Karl Rahner's most promising and trusted students in the late fifties and early sixties,[2] he had been Professor of Fundamental Theology at the University of Münster for some sixteen years, during which time he had become famous as one of the principal founders of what he called "the new political theology."[3] His magnum opus, *Faith in History and Society*, had been published two years earlier, and his importance in the West German Church had been demonstrated by his role in writ-

---

1. The details of the events surrounding Metz's vetoed appointment to the University of Munich are taken from John Allen's lucid account in John L. Allen, *Cardinal Ratzinger: The Vatican's Enforcer of the Faith* (New York: Continuum, 2000), 124–27.

2. Rahner had selected Metz to edit for republication both of Rahner's early foundational works, *Spirit in the World* and *Hearers of the Word*. Rahner had also chosen Metz to write pivotal entries (on "theology," "unbelief," and "the world," for instance) in the *Lexicon für Theologie und Kirche*, as well as the articles on apologetics and political theology in *Sacramentum Mundi*. Heinrich Fries himself, for whose chair in Munich Metz was being considered, had commissioned Metz to write entries on "freedom," "concupiscence," and "bodiliness" in *Handbuch theologischer Grundbegriffe*.

3. He named it thus to distinguish it in particular from the work of Carl Schmitt, a political theorist whose infamous "political theology" of the 1930s provided a "theological" justification of the Nazi state. Metz's vigorous attempts to differentiate his approach have never persuaded many of his critics. Indeed, it may very well be this association that lay behind Ratzinger's perception in the 1960s of "a conflict emerging that could go deep indeed" (cited in Moltmann's essay below, p. 54, n. 1).

ing the conclusions of the Synod of West German Bishops, *Unsere Hoffnung*.[4] He was clearly a rising star in German Catholic theology. Then Cardinal Ratzinger intervened. A little over a year apart in age, both Bavarians from "arch-Catholic" villages, Ratzinger and Metz had been colleagues at Münster before Ratzinger went to Tübingen, and then left academic theology to become Bishop of Regensburg. Metz and Ratzinger had been on good terms; indeed, Ratzinger had helped Metz secure his position in Münster. Now, as Archbishop of Munich, Ratzinger too was a star in the ascendant in the young papacy of John Paul II. Within two years he would be appointed the prefect of the Congregation for the Defense of the Faith, the position he still held when he came to Ahaus in 1998. Yet here, some two decades earlier, Ratzinger did something that, together with his actions in the German Bishops' Conference to remove Hans Küng's *missio canonica* to teach Catholic theology, was seen by many as a prelude to the policies he would implement in that powerful position. Under a provision of the concordat worked out between the Bavarian government and the Holy See in 1924, the local bishop had the right to veto the top choice for a given appointment to a faculty of Catholic theology. Ratzinger availed himself of this perquisite and prevailed on the Bavarian Minister of Culture to appoint Heinrich Döring instead of Metz.[5]

Ratzinger's intervention unleashed a storm of controversy, including a particularly strong, even vitriolic letter of protest from Metz's former teacher and mentor, Karl Rahner.[6] Metz himself

---

4. For the former title: Johann Baptist Metz, *Faith in History and Society*, 2nd English edition, translated and edited, with an introduction by J. Matthew Ashley (New York: Crossroad, forthcoming).

5. In a conversation with me in June of 2002, Metz pointed out that there was opposition to his appointment in the Bavarian Ministry of Culture as well as from the episcopal chancellery.

6. "Ich protestiere," *Süddeutsche Zeitung*, November 19, 1979. Allen gives a partial translation, *Cardinal Ratzinger*, 125f.

seemed content to let others protest on his behalf, and went on to continue his distinguished career in Münster.[7] Yet, because of this intervention, and because of Ratzinger's subsequent history of dealings with Catholic theologians (one thinks particularly of Leonardo Boff), and given the strong counterreaction of European theologians, shown, for instance, in the Cologne Declaration of 1989,[8] it is not difficult to understand the astonishment, and for many, even outrage, that greeted the news that Ratzinger and Metz would occupy the same stage in Ahaus.[9]

Two final notes on the translation itself: First, insofar as I believe responsible English theological usage should strive where possible to use inclusive language for human beings and for God, I have tried to do so in what follows, even though the German texts here translated do not follow that usage. Other than that, the only changes I have made were to find English translations of the German texts cited or quoted wherever possible. In general, I have used already existing English translations of quoted works, where I could find them. All biblical quotes are from the New Revised Standard Version. Second, I would like to recognize two of my colleagues who helped me with this translation. Professor Thomas Prügl provided invaluable assistance with a number of translation quandaries, as well as with background information on the German cultural and political scene. For Eveline Goodman-Thau's lecture, Professor Hindy Najman helped me find citations and quotations from the Mishnah, the Talmud, and the Hebrew Bible. My heartfelt

---

7. See his rather muted comments in "On My Own Behalf," *The Emergent Church: The Future of Christianity in a Postbourgeois World,* trans. Peter Mann (New York: Crossroad, 1987), 121–23.
8. Signed by over four hundred European theologians, including figures as important as Edward Schillebeeckx, Norbert Greinacher, Bernard Häring, Hans Küng, and Metz himself, the declaration criticized church policies on issues such as the autocratic appointment of bishops, draconian measures against theologians, and the steady "creep" of claims for magisterial infallibility. It was greeted with anger by Ratzinger. See Allen, *Cardinal Ratzinger,* 282f.
9. Hans Küng was particularly incensed.

thanks to both of them. Of course, the translation is still my own, as is responsibility for any errors in it.

J. Matthew Ashley
South Bend, Indiana
April 2003

Foreword

On October 27, 1998, on the occasion of his seventieth birthday, a group of Johann Baptist Metz's friends and students, along with the Seminar for Fundamental Theology at the University of Münster and the current events/cultural forum in Ahaus, held a theology meeting at the palace in Ahaus. Although the theme, "The End of Time? The Provocation of Talking about God," did not seem to be all that controversial, or promise to be particularly relevant, it brought unaccustomed attention to Ahaus—already notorious because of the protests over nuclear waste transport and storage and nuclear power in general.

There were reasons for this. No less a figure than the Prefect of the Vatican's Congregation for the Defense of the Faith, Cardinal Joseph Ratzinger, had promised to participate, and then showed up—to the anger of many who did not come. Was Johann Baptist Metz, the advocate of a critical left wing in theology and in the Church, really supposed to engage seriously with this controversial chief defender of the faith, and this in tense, touchy times in church politics?

Eveline Goodman-Thau, the Jewish philosopher of religion, and Jürgen Moltmann, the Protestant with strong convictions in liberation and political theology, were also there. So, it was an encounter between quite distinct actors, with differences shaped both religiously and confessionally. The morning belonged to the chief speakers, Ratzinger and Metz, who, after speaking, reacted briefly to one another's remarks. In the afternoon a panel discussion was held, moderated by Robert Leicht (of *Die Zeit*), beginning with longer statements by Moltmann and Goodman-Thau.

The theological "provocation" that the name of the meeting announced had already stirred people up even in the initial stages and led to passionate reactions, both in agreement and disagreement. Yet in the Royal Hall of the Ahaus Palace, as well as in front of a video transmission of the talks, an audience made up primarily of students was caught up for a day in theological reflection—now quietly analytical, now forceful, at times laborious. There the "provocation" consisted not least in how totally seriously the events were being taken—provocative for all those who had expected a grand spectacle of theological and ecclesial politics.

"Theology is a helper, a support in the struggle, not an end in itself" (Dietrich Bonhoeffer). It is a support in the struggle on behalf of tormented and suffering men and women. This, at any rate, is the credo of Johann Baptist Metz's political theology, and it was Metz who was to be honored at this meeting. But who are those who suffer and from what do they suffer? Here lies the real theological and ecclesial bone of contention. Is suffering to be contested, or is it not rather to be borne? Does not suffering have a meaning that is experienced in faith? And may one overlook, in people who are the suffering, the one who is suffering from the Church?

It is one of the defining features of political theology that it takes crises in the Church very seriously without exhausting itself in political appeals within the Church. When caught up in a reform movement, it is necessary to come to a reflective consensus about what church and what God we are supposed to be talking about anyway. What are these times and this society in which we live and work out our dreams for the Church, or express our fears about the Church?

"Prescinding from doctrinal differences (although certainly aware of them), it would be a good thing, particularly today, to start once again with the eschatology from which the Church and theology have always lived, and probably only by virtue of which will be able to survive." This is what our letter of invitation to Cardinal Ratzinger said. In the program for the meeting, therefore, talk about God was presented as a "message about time" and characterized in this way: "Is the forgetfulness of time and of misery—in which even catastrophes these days are aestheticized or mythically enspelled—the sign of a profound 'God-crisis' today? This also appears to be a threat for those people who have been left mercilessly abandoned to their illusions, repressions, and compensatory devices. Thus it is just as necessary as it is provocative to stick to the God of Israel, to God's commandments and promises, and to remember that time is bounded, even the Church's time, and that there is great urgency that men and women be responsible and exercise critical freedom, even in the Church and in theology."

It will do our talk about God good to change the coordinates within which it functions publicly, to make new encounters possible, and to gain a new perspective on the whole of theological discourse (including those areas held to be taboo) and on distortions and weak points in church politics. A first step toward this extraordinary and fundamentally theological interchange was taken at Ahaus. What is more, one could feel there the desire that this not be the last, but rather the first of a series of conversations, with other partners and under other conditions.

The echo in the media was enormous, not excluding the international press. It is true that the fact that the theological meeting in Ahaus could be recorded on the other side of the Atlantic as a "catholic event" need not be taken as speaking for the Symposium itself. But it does speak for the powerful attraction exercised by such an attempt to arrive at a consensus that crosses borders and divisions.

Foreword

However much theology can feel flattered for having "enjoyed" the public spotlight in this way, it hardly draws any profit thereby. Details are not necessarily appreciated on this level of "public" interest. Nuances are glossed over and distinctions overlooked. And although at times it has been reported in an extraordinarily clear and precise way, the greatest impact of the meeting at Ahaus continues to be on the headlines: "An Appalling Stroke of Good Fortune: Cardinal Ratzinger Fights Alongside the Theologian Johann Baptist Metz—Against Too Much Modernity" (*Die Zeit*); "Auschwitz Has Changed Theology: The Disciplinarian and the Rebel Act like Friends" (*Süddeutsche Zeitung*); "Trapped at Close Quarters: Ratzinger versus Metz over Cocktails (*Frankfurter Allgemeine Zeitung*); "Freedom, Evil, and Talk about God" (*Deutsche Tagespost*); "The Memory of Suffering or Metaphysics of Salvation" (*Neue Zürcher Zeitung*); "Time Travel Theology" (*Christ in der Gegenwart*); "Peace Offering Stirs New Debate" (*National Catholic Reporter*).

Given the media interest, and especially in view of the inconsistencies, the offhand quotes in the news, and the biased reviews, there is a demand for the texts themselves, for what was really said. Hence this documentation.[1] The greatest care has been taken to make the symposium intelligible as a forum for theological discussion and an experiment in church politics. The opening address, lectures, statements, and conclusions are reproduced in their entirety; the discussions have been edited slightly to make them flow more smoothly, but none of the words have been changed.

Tiemo Rainer Peters and Claus Urban
Münster and Ahaus, December 1998

---

1. Currently a book is being prepared on the thematic areas broached at Ahaus: *Jahrbuch Politische Theologie*, Band 3; *Befristete Zeit*, hrg. Jürgen Manemann (Münster: Lit Verlag, 1999).

Tiemo Rainer Peters

"*Why Do We Do Theology?*"

It is not exactly academic custom for Johann Baptist Metz to be sent for his birthday into the theological arena along with Cardinal Joseph Ratzinger, instead of letting him enjoy friendly congratulations and recognition, and, what is more, for him to be invited in the afternoon to take the stage set by the philosopher of religion Eveline Goodman-Thau and the theologian Jürgen Moltmann, from the Jewish and Reformation traditions, respectively, making it a bit uncomfortable for him, or so we hope.

The idea behind this meeting, steeped in conflict, came from those of us who belong to the circle of his students and friends. But when you get right down to it, he is himself "to blame." For if there is anything that Johann Baptist Metz has become "famous" for, it is that he always preferred unfamiliar settings to the well-trodden ways of proceeding, and always found the points of divergence more interesting than the consonances. He has helped us to see the beauty of the strange, the skewed, the unorthodox. The place where theology ought to get involved is the place where its subject matter—God and human beings—is really under threat; Metz has never valued or exercised a theology that fits in with what is particularly modern or modish at a given moment, no matter where and how. In this sense he has taught us and urged us to be

1

uncomfortable. Thus: this symposium in his honor; this theme; these participants.

The meeting refuses to comply with the rules of a certain "correctness" in theology and church politics. It is disconcerting for the protagonist of a new political theology to sit down together with the most influential critic of his theology: Cardinal Ratzinger. And critic is too weak a word: think of his prevention of Metz from taking the chair in fundamental theology in Munich in 1979. It is scandalous to bring together a passionate advocate of the theology of liberation with a powerful opponent of this liberation theology. And it is just as bewildering as it is suspicious in a time of notorious tensions between Rome and university theology to invite, of all people, the curial Cardinal responsible for the doctrine of the faith to faraway Ahaus and to carry on an academic discussion about God and time with him.

"The End of Time? The Provocation of Talking about God"— I hope that by the end of this meeting the theme will have been understood in all its urgency. I will not comment on anything in anticipation of the discussion. Only this: there is a pathos, if you will, a naïveté in our concept: the notion, that is, that theology is possible, and that it must not immediately obey this or that worldview, strategy, or even ecclesial politics. This is theology as the opportunity to open up the space in which the whole can still be discussed, without in so doing letting the differences become irrelevant or blurred. On the contrary: the differences can come into sharper focus the more faithfully theology is carried on, and "God" as a consequence is said. This too we know first and foremost from Metz.

We have invited many young theology students in order to make it possible for them in particular to experience theology as a project in which no taboos about what can be thought or who can meet are laid down, but just the opposite: a project in which every-one listens to the others. In short: theology as the condition of the possibility for liberating discourse. In this way there is more and more of a chance that, together with many diverse voices, those that put us in contact with God will not be repressed. What other reason is there for doing theology? Cardinal Ratzinger, you have the first word.

Joseph Cardinal Ratzinger

The End of Time

Romano Guardini recorded in his journal notes a brief encounter that at first glance cannot but seem completely inconsequential for him, the elderly man, but which got right to the heart of what he was grappling with at that time of his life. A boy met him in the English garden and asked him, "What time is it?" He wanted to know the time of day shown on a watch. But Guardini became lost in thought: "Indeed, what time is it? How late has it gotten at this hour of my life?"[1]

In the youth's harmless question and in the pensive melancholy of an old man, two concepts of time run up against each other; two dimensions of the phenomenon of time touch. First we have clock time, which in turn images and captures cosmic time and the motion of the earth as seen from the sun's position. But Guardini was thinking of the hour of his life that has its own course through the heavens, of his own time in which it had gotten late and in which the end was knocking at the door. It is quite reasonable to assume as well that for Guardini—someone who had reflected on modernity and its end, on how late it was in Europe's history and the world's in general—it took on the sense of a question about the

---

1. Guardini, *Stationen und Rückblicke: Berichte über mein Leben* (Mainz: Paderborn, 1995), 209. [In German the question "What time is it?" is *"Wie spät ist es?"* Literally translated it means "How late is it?"—*trans.*]

hour in history. Thus, in this entirely ordinary occurrence, something of the complexity of the phenomenon of time revealed itself: There is not simply "time"; there are quite different dimensions to time, which are no doubt related to one another and mutually interwoven, but which are also clearly distinguished from one another.

So whoever would ask about the end of time must first ask: What in general is this thing, time? Of course, a thorough consideration of this question would require an entire treatise of its own, which I cannot attempt here. But it is at least necessary to take some brief note of the essential levels of time, which can be made out in their outlines in reflecting on our little story. First, there is *cosmic time*, the rhythm of the course of the stars, which is reflected for us in the phenomenon of day and night and in the passage of the years, and from which comes the units that our clocks measure. Here again for us earthlings, two different systems are available for measuring time: lunar and solar time. The fact that both of these in turn have to be thought of in terms of the manifold cycles of the cosmos, in terms of a system in motion without any fixed point of reference, in terms, to be precise, of a relativistic system, points to the limits of our horizon and to the sort of geocentric perspective on our world that will necessarily always be a part of our understanding of time, no matter how much our horizons expand.

Within this cosmic time, which it would probably be better to call celestial time, we could distinguish between plants' time and animals' time, but we will have to leave this point to one side here. But we very much have to reflect on the time that is proper to human beings. First there is the individual's time, tracing an arc from birth to death, for which there is a very beautiful image in the old Latin version of Psalm 30:16: *"In manibus tuis tempora mea"*—"All of my times are in your hands." But one could also translate this: "My temples are in your hands" or "You have my temples in your hands."

A person's pulse beat is thus looked upon as the rhythm of his or her time, which once again is encompassed by the hands of God.

This time of the individual is integrated into the time of history, but history's time presents itself once again on different levels. There are local histories, the history of a people, of a cultural area, which, just like the history of an individual life, spans the arc from its emergence to its end. No one contests that there is an end to "time" in this case, just as there is for the individual person. But does human history as a whole have an end as well? Is the arc that is traced out by an individual's life and by particular realms of history also an image for history as a whole? Does it too have its path through the heavens, which necessarily leads to an end, or will ever-new cycles be inaugurated? And how is an end to be conceived? Simply as extinction, defeat, ruin, death—paralleling the death of the individual or a culture's dying out?

Or is it not precisely the sphere of an individual's life as well as that of local histories that suggests another idea to us? Every individual life has an impact that is woven in its own way into the whole of the rest of history, just as the lives of his or her ancestors have an impact on his life. A culture in decline still has an impact on the continuing course of history. Is the end of time, of the whole of history, only a ceasing, or is there even in this instance a kind of continuation—perhaps a judgment, a separation of the good and the evil in it?

These are the questions urged on us just by naming the different levels of time. But we will have to postpone treating them in order to bring some order to the problem. First, we have to consider the question of how the different layers of time are related to one another. It is clear that human beings are integrally woven into the cosmos and related to it. Yet is the cosmos also ordered toward the person, or is the vast world of the stars completely indifferent with regard to whether or not life has come into being somewhere, on some planet, and to whether or not intelligent beings exist? Is the cosmos neutral when it comes to human beings, so that their beginning and eventual end is finally a meaningless marginal phenomenon, which can just as well exist as not?

Does, therefore, the end of time concern only human beings and not the world? And if this were so, is the person finally only a cosmic phenomenon, or does not the person have a significance of his or her own? Over against "cosmocentrism" can there be a legitimate "anthropocentrism"? In this way, the question about the levels of times harbors the question about what the end of time can and cannot mean. The two questions, distinct in themselves, about how different times are ordered with respect to one another and about the beginning and the end, finally cannot be separated. Thus, while it is true that they always have to be treated separately, they also must be treated in conjunction with one another. In what follows, I would like to juxtapose the four ways of resolving these questions that I can see in intellectual history, and at the same time to relate them to one another, in order to glean from the mutual critiques they raise a perspective on the issues that confront us.

On the Aristotelian View of Time— Along with a Theological Variation on Aristotle

Aristotle drew a cosmocentrically oriented image of the world that continues to impress us for the clarity of his logic and the coherence of his vision. This image of the world is determined by the ordering of time and non-time. The cosmos itself is an everlasting movement of spheres that has neither beginning nor end. But this movement needs a motor, so to speak, that must itself be infinite but that cannot for its part be a movement. The unmoved mover is the unceasing energy for the all. Since it is unmoved, it stands outside of time, for time is based on movement. The absolutely unmoved, immutable, eternal is thus to be characterized in as radical a way as non-time. Time is bound to eternity, to non-time. Time depends on that which is non-time, draws from it its energy. Eternity, however, is not related to time, but stands utterly in itself. For otherwise it would itself be a movement, would itself be something relative, and could not long support that which is relative. The contingent postulates the non-contingent. But since this unmoved mover is by nature without beginning and end, time can then also always exist without a beginning or an end. Its temporality is based not on beginning and ending but on the unending existence of that which is self-moving. Time is nothing but movement and is defined by movement, just as eternity is defined by non-movement, by the sheer simplicity of being.[2]

The idea that eternity is non-time and that the nature of God is described in these terms has also had a great deal of influence on Christian thought. With that starting point, Thomas Aquinas taught that it would in principle be possible to combine a cosmos without beginning or end with Christian faith; it is only through a specific revelation that one knows that the world as creation has a beginning and as history has an end. But one cannot grasp this by a philosophical route, nor by any other ideas that are in themselves necessarily connected with faith in God.[3]

Above and beyond this quite compelling Aristotelian-Christian approach of St. Thomas's, there has been in our own times a strange continuation of the idea of eternity as non-time, one that

---

2. See, for example, D. J. Allan, *The Philosophy of Aristotle,* 2nd edition (Oxford: Oxford University Press, 1970), especially 35–39.

3. See M. Seckler, "Was heißt eigentlich 'Schopfung'? Zugleich ein Beitrag zum Dialog zwischen Theologie und Naturwissenschaften," *ThQ* 177 (1977): 161–88, especially 179ff.

has a bearing on our question. A broad cross section of theologies advocates the opinion that temporality is connected to bodiliness, and that as a consequence the movement of human beings from life into death is at the same time a movement out of time and into non-time—an idea, of course, that could have never arisen in the Aristotelian system. Thus, whoever leaves physically/biologically determined bodiliness behind could not enter into an interim phase of the expectation of the end of time. She would find herself completely outside of time in eternity, which is non-time. She would be standing beyond time. It would not be possible to think of judgment and the end of time as something still awaiting her, since this would mean reintroducing time elements where there is no time. Being there, where God is, in the non-time of eternity, one has arrived at the already-perfected world of the resurrection beyond history, since with God as wholly untemporal, everything is already perfected, and that which is still outstanding within time is already everlastingly present there. In this way history as time could placidly keep on going while on the other side, history is always already fulfilled. The suffering that is endured on the one side is on the other always already overcome in the definitive victory of God.[4]

Identifying eternity with non-time and locating everything non-physical on the level of non-time gives rise to a dualism of two worlds in which it seems to me that history loses all its seriousness.

---

4 See J. Ratzinger, *Eschatology: Death and Eternal Life* (Washington, DC: The Catholic University of America Press, 1988), particularly 107f. Admittedly, G. Greshake, who had given a forceful formulation of this position in his book *Auferstehung der Toten* (Essen, 1969), has since then modified the concept of "resurrection in death" in such a way as to take into account the problem that we are addressing here, when, for instance, he says, "Therefore the final fulfillment of the individual is only possible in the fulfillment of the whole, and talking about a resurrection on the last day proves to be absolutely necessary and meaningful. Neither need this way of speaking reject the concept of a resurrection in death" (*Lexicon für Theologie und Kirche*, third edition, I:1204f.).

Joseph Cardinal Ratzinger

While here we think we are slaving away in history, there it is already over. The end of history has nothing to do with history itself, but rather exists in that place where there isn't any history anyway.

I must confess that I continue to find this dualism unintelligible, however broadly it is being accepted today with the talk about resurrection in death, which surely presupposes precisely these ideas of death as a movement out of time to a place where everything that appears to us as the future is already the nontemporal present. One thing is of course quite clear: To clarify the concept of *time*, it is also necessary to clarify the concept of *eternity*, as well as the distinction of levels of time. Time is not just a physical phenomenon. The existence of time does not only depend on the movement of the stars; there is also movement in the realm of the heart, of the spirit. And that is why it is necessary to ask whether God's relationship to the world and to time can be described simply with the concept of non-time. Something that is altogether logical and correct in Aristotle's cosmic system becomes inconsistent when one connects it with the Christian concept of God, in which God, who establishes history, enters into a covenant—and this even to the point of becoming a man himself. Naturally one cannot ascribe the same mode of temporality to God as one does to human beings interwoven into the cosmos, or even to human beings who have left bodiliness behind in death. If in this I am disagreeing with a Christian Aristotelianism, so too am I disagreeing with Oscar Cullman, who, in an understandable reaction against Aristotelianism and Platonism, thought that biblically speaking, God too belongs to time, and who calls everything time and history in the same way.[5] Emil Brunner's suggestion seems to me

5. See Oscar Cullman, *Christ and Time: The Primitive Christian Conception of Time and History* (Philadelphia: Westminster, 1964), esp. 61–68.

more apt: from the perspective of a Christian image of God, God's eternity should be defined not as timelessness but as power over time.[6]

The God of the Bible is no power in repose, holding the world in motion without being affected itself. When Dante names God the *"amor…che muove il sole e le altre stelle"* ([the Love that moves the sun and other stars], *Paradiso* 33:144), then we can certainly make out the Aristotelian vision in the background, but something new is being said with the concept of amor: the idea of a relationship that accepts the other within itself and lets itself be accepted by that other. The image of hands encircling time, and in so doing becoming contemporaneous with it, seems to me the best one for depicting both God's relationship to time and, at the same time, God's superiority over time. We have been too long within the Aristotelian conceptual framework.

Rethinking the essence of eternity, based on the insights and experiences of Christian faith, seems to me to be in large measure still an unfinished task. Once one takes it up then the strong cosmocentrism of the Aristotelian vision breaks apart of its own accord, since then it is no longer just the phenomenon of physical movement that counts, but also the movement of the spirit; and history and human beings thus receive their proper status.

Time from the Perspective of the Natural Sciences

Whoever speaks of "the end of time" may be speaking anthropocentrically, yet he or she cannot neglect looking at the cosmos, which is an essential element in the construction of time for human

---

6. See Emil Brunner, *The Christian Doctrine of God, Dogmatics*, Volume 1, trans. by Olive Wyon (Philadelphia: Westminster, 1950–79), 256–71.

beings.[7] This means taking a look at what the natural sciences say. It seems to me that in themselves the natural sciences suggest a model of a cosmos without beginning or end. The evolutionary view of the world stands in contrast to this, of course, such that one has to presume some kind of a beginning in one form or another. The law of entropy makes one think of a kind of approach to a final state under the laws of nature, a kind of end to time. How much this is so in its particulars is also open to discussion. In this kind of vision, beginning and end are purely cosmic phenomena; at best, human beings using up the world might accelerate the onset of entropy, the motionlessness of the macroscopic realm, and thus a kind of cosmological end to time.

Ever since human beings have penetrated to the roots of cosmic energy, have been able to unleash nuclear explosions and nuclear fusion, and with DNA have apparently taken hold of the key to life, these cosmic visions have begun to take on anthropological features. Human beings could themselves bring about the end of time, a catastrophe of cosmic proportions. The human spirit, this uncanny product of development, would then be the destructive force that is able to snuff out and destroy, not the cosmos, to be sure, but certainly the evolution of life. Then what we would have would be a kind of self-destruction of evolution. Evolution as a whole would look like something ultimately accidental, something that also cancels itself out with a certain necessity, leaving behind in the end only a few scorch marks by which to remember its processes. Basically, then, human beings, with their destructive power, would really only be a product of nature,

---

7. On the questions addressed here, see *Christlicher Glaube in moderner Gesellschaft,* Teilband 3 mit Beiträgen von K. Rawer, K. Rahner, St. N. Boeshard, B. Hassenstaein, K. Meyer-Abich (Freiburg: 1989); R. J. Russel, W. R. Stoeger, G. V. Coyne (eds.), *Physics, Philosophy, and Theology* (Notre Dame, IN: University of Notre Dame Press, 1998).

a mistake of evolution, through which it comes to an end. Humanity's time would look rather like Saturn, who swallowed his own children.

Disturbing visions like these, which arise from a wholly naturalistic view of being, cannot perhaps be refuted on strictly rational grounds. Or is the cry of opposition, of protest against the meaninglessness, in which suffering would be nothing more than something naturally necessary and justice a meaningless concept, not itself a reality that forbids us to tarry with visions like these?

Faith in Progress

Up until the visions of catastrophes surfaced, following the horrors of the bombing of Hiroshima and Nagasaki, the prevailing model was a different one: progress, "eternally," as Kant put it.[8] I think that along with the primordial fear of catastrophe, the idea of progress is still the dominant scheme for history in our contemporary consciousness. People are certain that the Middle Ages were dark. They know that with the Enlightenment came a growing freedom and liberation for men and women. Day in and day out people experience technological progress, and even those who see its dangers see all the same the growing possibilities that it bestows on humanity. All of this is connected with the image of the evolutionary cosmos, so that the mounting processes of nature together with the progressive development of the human spirit seem to guarantee that progress is reality's fundamental law, despite all the setbacks and threats.

---

8. See his *Vorlesungen über Metaphysik* 28/1, 446. [English translation: Immanuel Kant, *Lectures on Metaphysics*, translated and edited by Karl Ameriks and Steve Naragon, The Cambridge Edition of the Works of Immanuel Kant (Cambridge: Cambridge University Press, 1997), 293]. See the important article "Fortschritt" by J. Ritter, in J. Ritter (ed.) *Historisches Wörterbuch der Philosophie* II:1032–59; here, 1048.

Joseph Cardinal Ratzinger

One can probably say that as the two great philosophical creations of modern consciousness, both the liberal and the Marxist image of the world, are ultimately shaped by the idea of progress, which, of course, connects them with a strange eschatological consciousness: Finally, at some point in the dialectic of human history, society's perfected state will inevitably arise, in which nature and freedom are wholly reconciled, freedom will have become human beings' natural state, as it were, and thus moral excellence and a fulfilled life will be shared by all. One need not think of an end of time here.

Of course, if the image of perfected freedom, of a perfect society somehow means something like a *fulfillment of time*, then at that point the goal of historical movement has certainly been attained, which seems to exclude the possibility of any further meaningful historical development. To me this seems to some degree to be fundamentally the case for Hegel's vision of history, as well as Marx's. But then the questions arises: What kind of "time" is this, really? And what sort of freedom is it that no longer falls, but rather stands from generation to generation in all its fullness? Then the question unavoidably arises that Adorno so clearly posed: What kind of reconciliation is it that only counts for those who come after? What about us? What about the victims of injustice throughout history?

These questions are also valid ones for the Christian variant of this faith in progress that Teilhard de Chardin developed.[9] He described the cosmos as a process of upward development, as a journey of unification. From the very simple, this journey leads to ever greater and more complex units in which multiplicity is not canceled out but integrated into a growing synthesis, culminating in the Noosphere, where spirit and its understanding comprehend the whole, and everything is integrated into a kind of living

---

9. See N. M. Wildiers, "Teilhard de Chardin," in *Lexicon für Theologie und Kirche,* IX, 1341f.

14

organism. Based on Ephesians and Colossians, Teilhard envisages Christ as the energy that drives toward the Noosphere, an energy that finally incorporates everything in its fullness.

This impressive vision, in which the Eucharist appears as the anticipation of the transformation and divination of matter, as the compass needle orienting the cosmic movement, has to face all those questions that have to be posed to the idea of progress in general. For Teilhard all of evolution's terrible aspects and so too, finally, all of history's atrocities, are inevitable mishaps in the process of upward movement toward the definitive synthesis. You just cannot have the experiment in which nature searches out its way, so to speak, without failures, which in the end would be the unavoidable price of the ascent. Thus, in the end human beings in their suffering appear as the material for evolution's experiment, the world's injustices as mishaps that you have to reckon for on such a journey. Humanity is subordinated to the cosmic process; but this is precisely when the age-old question that the Psalms put to God acquires a new urgency: "What are human beings, that you are mindful of them?" (Ps 8:5).

Or is it that we have to reckon our sense of the direct relation of each and every person to God to be arrogance, and bow before the majesty of the cosmos, to the Godhead of evolution? Or is it that there is a God who is greater than the cosmos and before whom one single person is greater than the whole silent cosmos? Clearly all of this presses the God question upon us. The questions about time, about its endlessness, and about its end merge with the question about God.

Here, not far from Münster, a short excursus seems apropos at this point, a brief memory of Josef Pieper, who from World War II on pursued the theme of "the end of time," studying what Thomas Aquinas said about the Antichrist. For the winter semes-

15

ter of 1948–49 he announced a lecture on "The End of Time in the Philosophy of History," reaping thereby the astonishment of his colleague, Heinrich Stolz, as well as the stunned amazement of the rector, Friedrich Meineckte.[10] The conflict with Teilhard de Chardin came when Pieper spoke in Paris in 1951 on "The Hope of the Martyrs." His thesis was that one should decline to talk about hope "if there be no hope for those who allowed themselves to be killed for the sake of truth and of justice, and who, at any rate, found themselves in a 'hopeless' place—imprisoned, isolated, made objects of contempt, and, above all, silenced."[11]

Only five years after Teilhard's death Pieper learned of a letter that the French Jesuit had penned "in the passion of the moment" right after the lecture, which he had attended. Pieper had said in the lecture (it isn't written down anywhere) "that with the victory of reason or of justice human history, looked at from within time, will simply come to an end."[12] In his letter Teilhard called this approach to the question "defeatist": There is, after all, something completely different that is very important, "namely, the futural power of a humanity that is still 'young,' when looked at 'biocosmically' from the perspective of its evolutionary potential." In his memoirs Pieper criticized this mingling of evolution and history: "One can only talk meaningfully about the witness of blood," he said in this regard, "in the field of history, whereas evolution knows no martyrs."[13]

10. J. Pieper, *Noch nicht aller Tage Abend: Autobiographische Aufzeichnungen 1945-64* (München: Kösel, 1979), 56f.
11. Ibid., 112.
12. Ibid., 112f.
13. Ibid., 113.

The Classical Theological Model

This clash of evolutionary and historical thinking alone invites us to briefly consider the image of history and of time that has developed in the core of the Christian tradition. It is common today to contrast the Christian understanding of time as linear to the cyclical understandings of time in the philosophy of antiquity. From the perspective of medieval theology, and probably for the Fathers too, one cannot demarcate things schematically in this way. For medieval theology took over a scheme for history that had been passed down from antiquity and that characterized creation's time with the two directional elements *"exitus–reditus,"* or "turning outward" *(Auskehr)* and "turning inward" *(Einkehr)*. This is, thus, to think in terms of a kind of circular movement.

Thomas Aquinas, for example, says in this regard that "circular movement is the most perfect of all movements since a return to the origins occurs in it. If the universe is to attain its final perfection then creatures must return to their origin."[14] He connects this in an impressive way with faith in the incarnation of the Son of God in Jesus Christ, in which he sees the turning point, so to speak, in the circular movement of history and of the cosmos:

> The mystery of the Incarnation is signified with the image of turning rivers back....The rivers are the natural goods that God has infused into creatures....But the place at which the rivers originate is God Godself....The human being is like the horizon and the boundary, as it were, between spiritual and corporeal

---

14. Thomas Aquinas, *Summa contra gentiles*, II, 46; see Jean-Pierre Torrell: *Saint Thomas Aquinas. Volume 1: The Person and His Work*, trans. Robert Royal (Washington, DC: Catholic University of America Press, 1996), 154f.

nature and he is like the mean between both. For this reason all the rivers of natural goods turn back to their origin when human nature is united with God's nature through the mystery of the incarnation.[15]

With the image of history as a circle from origin to home-coming, the turning point of which is God's incarnation, Thomas has taken up a human paradigm and christianized it.[16] For Thomas, as for medieval thought in general, the whole history of the cosmos and humanity appears as a great circular movement. This paradigm engenders a certain theological anthropocentrism (taking this word quite literally) to the extent that the human, to which God unites Godself, is the center of the movement, and this movement arrives at its goal through humanity. In nature religions and in many non-Christian philosophies the cosmos and history appear as a movement that is forever repeating itself.

Properly understood, the contrast between these two per-spectives is not as exclusive as it might appear at first glance. For even for the Christian view of the world many small cycles of indi-vidual life are inscribed in the one great cycle of history that moves from *exitus* to *reditus*. These individual lives carry the greater rhythm of the whole within themselves and continually actualize it anew, thus giving it the power of its movement. And in the one great cycle, the many life cycles of different cultures and historical com-

15. Thomas Aquinas, *Liber Sententiarum* III, Prologue. For Bonaventure's position on this issue see Joseph Ratzinger, *Die Geschichtstheologie des heiligen Bonaventura*, 2nd edition (St. Ottilien: EOS Verlag Erzabtel, 1992), 140–48. Eng. trans., *The Theology of History in Saint Bonaventure*, trans. Zachary Hayes (Chicago, IL: Franciscan Herald Press, 1971).

16. The following discussion is taken in large part from a book on which I am currently at work, "Introduction to the Spirit of the Liturgy" [this book appeared subsequently: *The Spirit of the Liturgy*, trans. John Saward (San Francisco: Ignatius Press, 2000)].

munities are inscribed, in which the drama of birth, rise, and end is played out ever anew. In them the mystery of the beginning is repeated again and again; however, processes of decline and the end of time happen in them too, which can in its own way prepare the grounds for a new beginning. The sum total of all these cycles mirrors the one greater cycle; all of these cycles are related to one another and intermesh with one another.

There is another important pair of alternatives, which first developed in the contrast between Christian faith and non-Christian philosophy. With Plotinus, for example, and then in a closely related way in the Gnostic philosophies, *exitus*, by virtue of which there is any non-divine being at all, appears not as a going forth but as a *Fall*, as a ruinous fall from the heights of divinity, a fall which, something like the law of gravity, drove things to ever greater depths and into an ever greater distance from the divine. This means that non-divine being is in itself and as such fallen being; finitude is itself already a kind of sin, something negative that has to be healed by being drawn back into the infinite. Turning homeward—*reditus*—now consists just in this: The fall is intercepted at its deepest point and the trajectory is directed upward. In the end the "sin" of not being God is annulled and in this sense God becomes "all in all."

The journey of *reditus* means redemption, and redemption means liberation from finitude, which as such is the real burden of our existence. Gazing up to the divine turns into becoming aware of the fall; it is, as it were, the moment of contrition of the Prodigal Son, the turning anew to one's origins. Since according to this philosophy being and knowledge coincide, to look anew on the beginning is at the same time already to rise anew in that direction. Worship as looking up toward that which is prior to and beyond all being is essentially knowledge, and, as knowledge, it is movement, homecoming, and redemption.

Ideas like these exercise a tremendous fascination and it seems very easy to identify them with the Christian message. "Original sin," for example, so difficult to understand otherwise, becomes identical with the fall into the finite, and it is also then easy to see how it is inherent to everything that is stuck in the cycle of finitude. One makes sense of redemption as a liberation from the burden of finitude, and so on. What is important for our question is that from such a perspective time belongs together with finitude, since it is a product of the fall and is revoked in the new ascent. At the same time, of course, the finite time of the ongoing fall continues to exist, and for those who do not ascend, it becomes an empty and endless cycle.

In contrast to this, Christian thought has strongly distinguished two movements in the circle of *exitus* and *reditus*. *Exitus* is not primarily a fall from the infinite, the splitting of being and thereby the cause of all the world's misery; rather, *exitus* is to begin with something completely positive: the free creative act of God whose positive will is that there be created beings as something good in contrast to God, from which the response of freedom and love can come back to God. This is why non-divine being is not in itself already something negative, but the opposite: the positive fruit of the divine will. It is not rooted in a fall but in the positing of God who is good and who creates what is good. The act of being on the part of God that effects created being is an *act of freedom*. To this extent the principle of freedom is present in being itself from the ground up.

The *exitus*, or, better, the free creative act of God, does in fact aim at *reditus*; but this does not mean that created being is revoked. Rather, it means that the coming-into-its-own of the creature as an autonomous creature answers back in freedom to the love of God, accepts its creation as a command to love, so that a dialogue of love begins—that entirely new unity that only love can create. In it the being of the other is not absorbed, not annulled, but rather becomes wholly what it is precisely in giving itself. What results is a unity that is higher than the unity of elementary particles that can no longer be separated. This *reditus* is a "homecoming," but it does not cancel out creation but fully gives it its ultimate validity. This is the Christian idea of "God being all in all."

But the whole thing is connected with freedom, and the freedom of the creature is now the thing that bends back the positive *exitus* of creation, indeed, that disintegrates into fall, into the will to non-dependence, into saying no to *reditus*. Now love is understood as dependence and is rejected; in its place comes *autonomy* and self-sufficiency: to exist only from oneself and in oneself; to be a god *sui generis*. Thus the bow of *exitus* to *reditus* breaks apart. There is no longer a will to turn back inward, and it proves impossible to rise up by one's own power. That is why the process of turning back has to be set in motion by a power to heal, by a loving transformation of a broken freedom in a way of reconciling it that one passively endures. Precisely because all of this revolved around going it on one's own (*Selbersein*), around not needing the other, a part of the process, then, is being turned toward the other, who must rescue me from the snare that I can no longer undo on my own.

Now redemption requires a redeemer. The Fathers found this expressed in the parable of the lost sheep. For them this sheep, which is trapped in the thornbush and does not know how to get back anymore, is an image of people in general, who no longer come out of their bramble thicket and who cannot find the way to God on their own anymore either. The shepherd who finds it and carries it home is for them the Logos itself, the eternal Word, the eternal meaning of the cosmos that dwells in the Son of God, who himself sets off toward us and now takes the sheep upon his shoulder, which means he assumes human nature and as the God-man carries the creature, man, back home again. This is how the turn

21

back inward (*Einkehr*) becomes possible that gives a homecoming (*Heimkehr*). The saving turning point happens in the form of the cross of Christ, the love that gives itself away in death. This love is an act of new creation, which restores creation to its proper integrity. The sharing in this "pasch" of Christ, in this, his "passing over" from the divine to the human, from death to life, to the union of God and man, is consummated in the Liturgy.

According to this view time essentially has to do with *freedom*. It is a movement of freedom. It originates from God's creative freedom, which first prepares a space for freedom by means of the cosmic movement: The cosmos is not neutral when it comes to human beings. Human beings are not beggarly parasites of being; rather, the cosmos is created with freedom in mind, a freedom that takes up its inner trajectories and alone can bring them to their goal. For the homecoming that is the goal of its movement can only happen as a freedom that gives itself back and finds itself completely in so doing. Therefore, neither is this homecoming now a reabsorption of time into non-time; rather, it is the way that time becomes definitive. Its end is not dissolution but a way of continuing in existence, an illuminated freedom that finds its definitive state in the fusion of truth and love. It receives the cosmos that is related to it and belongs intimately to it, in such a way that the cosmos becomes "a new heaven and a new earth."

Of course, we cannot forget that there is a *risk to freedom* and all its consequences, as has been impressed on us by Auschwitz, that most terrible of the signs of this reality, which no optimism can talk or think its way around. The question of whether this has made the risk of freedom too high, its price too dear—whether it really would have been better for it not to have existed—is beyond our limits, beyond our horizon, and beyond the limits of our ability to understand. What holds here is what man said in God's presence at the end of the Book of Job: "See, I am of small account; what shall I answer you? I lay my hand on my mouth....I had heard of you by the hearing of the ear, but now my eye sees you; therefore I despise myself and repent in dust and ashes" (Job 40:4, 42:5f.).

In any event, we have to reckon with the fact that there is a failed freedom, unreconciled and irreconcilable, the irrevocable evil—a negative entropy of the spirit, so to speak, which "rigidifies" from below, which misuses the time that is given to it and leaves it a wreck. On the other hand, however, the central assertion of New Testament faith is that there is the possibility that fallen freedom and misused time can be taken hold of and reconciled in a *love* that takes its place, so that the wounds of injustice and of evil become signs of peace in the suffering that shoulders them. The homecoming, of which the Apocalypse speaks at the end of time, is no idyll, but rather presupposes the struggle against evil, injustice, and hatred. It entails a new action on God's part, going beyond creation, since only an infinite love, with its compassion, is strong enough to overcome hostility and make love credible again in the face of the fear of being dependent and the craving for the autonomy that, seemingly, is the only appropriate way for freedom to take. Only a God who leaves behind the distant position of creator and lord, even taking on the dependency of a slave, who does the servant's work of washing feet, only this God and his love have the power to take hold of the cosmos of freedom and to empower love as genuine autonomy, as true freedom. All of this may strike non-believers as naive or mythological, but how could the audacity of God not seem mythological to our emancipated rationality?

I already said earlier that both the liberal and the Marxist visions of the definitive reconciliation of freedom and natural necessity are riven with contradictions and, above all, they put past time behind them as the mere opening act to that which is definitively valid, a prelude which, in either case, offers no real promise to the living and the dead. With the Christian hope that was just suggested, can we come up with some idea of time gathered up into a final definitive state, a state in which it is not revoked but finds the valid way for it to continue to exist? I think that our reason can derive some help from the concept of *memory*. Men and women can interiorize the time that is passing by, give to it a continuing existence on a new level in which, on the one hand, it ceases as a time that passes, but yet, on the other hand, is given a continuing existence, a sort of eternity.

The Christian tradition has seen in the self-gift of Christ, in his "sacrifice," the genuine model for how time can be carried over into a new, fulfilled mode of existence, brought to an end and definitively validated at the same time. This gift occurs in time. As such it is in the first instance a temporal act, but one which in the giving of self over to the Father, transcends time and at the same time draws time into itself. Something greater than time ripens within time, so that time's end becomes at the same time its fulfillment. The external act of the crucifixion passes away; it exists in the *ephapax* of the unrepeatable. But the inner act, although bound to time, in exiting time becomes something perennial, a reality in which history can take its origin and find its end.

In this way it could very well be this central point in world history, its turning toward the *reditus* that helps us to understand what the end of time can mean positively. The theme of "God and time" could probably also be taken up once more based on considerations of this kind. From this perspective can we not have some inkling of how God is both in time and beyond it at the same time? The way that love internalizes time and is embraced by eternity can give us some sense of God's relationship to time and sovereignty over time.

One thing will have become clear: The question "What is time?" becomes most radical in the question about time's end. But whoever investigates the beginning and end of time must also ask what there is outside of and above time. That then decides the answer about the nature of time and about its beginning and its end. Therefore, the question about time is inseparably connected to the God question, which, when all is said and done, is a question of a rationally responsible free decision, and, to this extent, is a question that is at the same time completely temporal and also one that transcends time. The way we are able to understand time depends on the way we see God, on a "yes" or "no" to God. And it is not only the way we understand time that depends on this, but also how we are able to appropriate time in our actions, or squander it. Just as much as the question of time, the question of God is finally not a theoretical question, but rather the question of the *praxis* of one's life.

Johann Baptist Metz

God: Against the Myth of the Eternity of Time

A First Appraisal

The nature of this occasion suggests a particular starting point—that is to say, one with personal overtones. Seventy years old, I have been doing theology for decades, and yet I have the impression that I am still very much at the beginning, that at any rate I have hardly even said what is most important and that I still owe too many answers. Is this due only to me, to my own impotence, or is it not really also a function of theology itself, theology not as this or that, but as the ever-renewed risk of trying to talk about God? Surely God is not a problem in the technical sense that is solved and can then be laid to rest *ad acta*. Neither, therefore, is theology your usual method for solving problems. Its answers do not simply silence the questions which are being answered or make them go away; rather, they sharpen them. Whoever, for example, formulates talk about the God of Abraham, Isaac, and Jacob in such a way that it is no longer possible to hear in it the sighs of Job— and his plaintive cry of "How long?"—is not doing theology, but mythology. Whoever hears the message of Christ's resurrection in such a way that in it the cry of the son forsaken by God falls silent, is not hearing the Gospel, but a myth for the victors.

We cannot construct a common understanding of God based on just any image of God that we might ("postmodernly") come up with, none of which have any tolerance for negativity, for unconsoled pain. Rather, a common understanding turns on the image of God given in the biblical traditions. Do we really take the irreducible, painful dialectic of this image of God seriously? This is what I wonder when I hear the oh-so-positive imagery used for God in preaching today, in which it is only the "love" of God that is talked about. Of course, I also ask myself this when I read that critics say it has only been the Church that has painted a dark image of God in order to terrify people and keep them down. No, it is already life itself that presents us with this dark image of God and that a mature faith must not simply paper over, but before which it has to hold its ground—even if that be with the creature's wordless sigh. How narcissistic would a faith have to be that, faced with this misery and this abysmal suffering in creation, in God's creation, knew only of rejoicing and not of a crying out before the dark face of God?

In this context too permit me a reference to my theological biography. I belong to that generation of Germans that slowly— probably much too slowly—had to learn to conceive of itself as a generation "after Auschwitz," and to take this into account in the way that it did theology. Understanding Auschwitz as a critical interrogation of one's own theology is anything but a transparent instrumentalizing of this catastrophe, anything but a dubious attempt to stylize it as a "negative myth." Rather, for me, this catastrophe signals a horror for which I have found neither a place nor a language in theology, a horror which bursts all the familiar ontological and metaphysical certainties in our talk about God and restricts theology to using those "weak" concepts and categories of thought that are sensitive to the situation—in the style of a new, secondary nominalism, as it were. Has Christian talk about God used categories for looking at history that are possibly much too "strong"? Categories that have far too quickly covered over all the wounds, decay, and catastrophes in history, and spared its logic the pain of remembering? Must not theology be convinced, at least today, that it is forbidden to think about Christianity's identity like one of Plato's timeless ideas, or—in a fashionable shift of focus from history to psychology—like a Gnostic myth of redemption that is far removed from history?

Christian talk about God and God's Christ is not based on a metaphysics of salvation that is blind to situations and devoid of memories; it is itself shaped by a historical remembrance and can only be responsible for its talk about God in critical correspondence with the situation that presses itself on theology at a given time. This is the only way that it can know and communicate what it is talking about when it says, "God." Neither can talk about God simply be something that is ecclesiologically enciphered. Either the God of the Church's message is a theme for humanity or it is no theme at all. This, at any rate, is how I read and understand the First Vatican Council's doctrines concerning the so-called "natural knowledge of God." The God proclaimed by the Church is neither the Church's private property nor faith's; for we have to reckon with the lightning bolt of God (this is precisely what we learn from the Bible) in every region of human experience and language. Thus, the sphere of the Church is really too narrow and too small to accommodate the full breadth and depth of the God that it proclaims.

Two Messages about Time

In order to discuss the provocation of God talk in our situation, I will make use of a mediation—the meditation offered by the question concerning time. In the end the biblical traditions' message about God needs to be heard as a message about time, more precisely, as a message about bounded time, about a time that has a finale. All of its statements about God bear a temporal stamp, a stamp of the end times. This means that this message about God is based on an elementary structuring of time by memory, by that memory of suffering in which the name of God is narrated and attested as a salvific name, as time's imminent end. This *time with a finale*, this oriented time, unknown to either the Greek-Mediterranean or the Near Eastern cultural worlds,[1] became the root of the understanding of the world as history and marks the opening act of the historical consciousness, which subsequently had such a lasting impact on the spirit of European modernity, and this, in fact, even long after modernity had, in its secularity and its critique of religion, rejected the theological and metaphysical substance of this way of thinking about time.

Of course, since then a momentous shift or transformation in the way time is thought about has come to stand in the foreground of "the spiritual situation of the age" (a phrase, of course, that goes back to Karl Jaspers, and which we shouldn't make too much of here), constituting something like an elementary "spiritual rupture." It can be illuminated in an abbreviated way in terms of some names from German intellectual history. For Marx and Hegel, for example, time, history, and human beings still had a goal that could be reflexively determined: something speculatively transparent for Hegel, and the subject of political struggle for Marx. In Nietzsche, on the

---

1. The qualitative caesura found in the Jewish Apocalypses in comparison with the approaches taken in antiquity in the East is stressed even in Norman Cohn, *Cosmos, Chaos and the World to Come: The Ancient Roots of Apocalyptic Faith* (New Haven, CT: Yale University Press, 1993).

other hand, there no longer is any finale, not even, as he explicitly emphasized, a "finale into nothingness."[2]

Correctly understood, Nietzsche's message about the "death of God" is a message about time. His revocation of God's dominion is the proclamation of the dominion of time, of the elemental, relentless, and unfathomable majesty of time. "God is dead." In all passing away, what is left is time itself: more eternal than God, more deathless than all the gods. It is the time which never begins or ends, the time which knows no bounds and no goals: *eternal time*.[3]

Now the "new man" becomes the "pilgrim without a goal," the "nomad without an itinerary," the "vagabond" in a Dionysian key, for whom all the highlights in things and relationships have vanished. He becomes the "flexible man" who drifts off goallessly. All of these descriptions do not at all arise from a culturally pessimistic theology, but rather from contemporary social theories.[4] Now this "new man" is less and less his own memory and more and more his own experiment, and nothing more. All the exigencies that come to us from our pasts are transformed into continually open options. And now the mystery of his redemption no longer finds its roots (as the well-known saying from the Talmud suggests) in remembering, but in forgetting, in a new cult of amnesia. Nietzsche, who long ago displaced Marx and Hegel in

---

2. Friedrich Nietzsche, *Werke in drei Bänden* (München, 1958), i.a., here III: 853. [This is from the *Nachlaß*, Nietzsche's unpublished notebooks from the 1880s. For an English translation in this instance, see *Nietzsche: Writings from the Late Notebooks* (Cambridge: University of Cambridge Press, 2003), 118—trans.]

3. Friedrich Nietzsche, *Werke*, Bd III, 456: "Die Zeit ewig." [This passage from the *Nachlaß* was not included among the selections translated in *Writings from the Late Notebooks*—trans.]

4. See Z. Bauman, *Postmodern Ethics* (Cambridge, MA: Blackwell, 1993); R. Sennet, *The Corrosion of Character: The Personal Consequences of Work in the New Capitalism* (New York: W. W. Norton, 1998).

the background of this situation, connected his "new way of life" to the triumph of this cultural amnesia.

> But in the case of the smallest and the greatest happiness, it is always just one thing alone that makes happiness happiness: the ability to forget....Anyone who cannot forget the past entirely and set himself down on the threshold of the moment, anyone who cannot stand, without dizziness or fear, on one single point like a victory goddess, will never know what happiness is....[5]

Thus, in the background of the spiritual situation of our age there are two messages about time opposing one another. One, which has its origins in the biblical traditions and has had a profound impact on modernity, is a message of time with a finale. The other is a message of time without finale, in short, of the eternity of time, which was already articulated in an enciphered form in the early Greek myths of the eternal return of the same, and which now, in its postmodern version, so to speak, is spelled out so prominently in Nietzsche.[6]

---

5. Friedrich Nietzsche, *Unfashionable Observations*, translated with an afterword by Richard T. Gray, *Complete Works of Friedrich Nietzsche*, vol. 2 (Stanford, CA: Stanford University Press, 1995), 88f.

6. On the connection between Nietzsche and Heidegger's project to temporalize ontology, as well as their significance for the fundamental question about "God and time," see J. B. Metz, *Zum Begriff der neuen Politischen Theologie: 1967–1997* (Mainz: Grünewald, 1997), 160ff. See also "Theology versus Polymythicism: A Short Apology for Biblical Monotheism," in J. B. Metz, *A Passion for God: The Mystical Political Dimension of Christianity*, translated and edited with an introduction by J. Matthew Ashley (Mahwah, NJ: Paulist Press, 1998), 72–92; "Time without a Finale," in J. B. Metz and J. Moltmann, *Faith and the Future: Essays on Theology, Solidarity, and Modernity*, with an introduction by Francis Schüssler Fiorenza (Maryknoll, NY: Orbis Books, 1995), 79–86; "Gotteskrise," in J. B. Metz et al., *Diagnosen zur Zeit* (Düsseldorf: Patmos, 1994), 76–92.

Johann Baptist Metz

God and Time
(or, a brief apology for the apocalyptic legacy)

The theme of "God and time" that this presses upon us demands a rapprochement with a biblical legacy that these days is often proscribed or rendered harmless, and which, in the way that it *is* commonly used, is for the most part entirely misunderstood: the legacy of apocalypticism.

Yet if one tarries a moment longer with the biblical apocalypticism's texts and images, and bears up against them for just a tiny bit longer than the modern consensus would appear to allow, then one can recognize that this apocalypticism is not about a speculation divorced from history, not about zealously sharpened imaginings of disaster, not about a catastrophe-crazed claim about the point in time for the world's finale. Rather, it has to do with a pictorial commentary on the ultimate nature of the world's time itself. For this apocalyptic language God is the mystery of time that has not yet been uttered, a mystery still outstanding. "Sentinel, what of the night?"....The sentinel says: "Morning comes, and also the night. If you will inquire, inquire; come back again" (Isa 21:11–12).

By all important accounts Israel, gifted in being *here,* caught up in the world, did not believe in and think about its saving God in an otherworldly way. It did not believe in and think about God as time's hereafter, but rather as time's end, oncoming and setting its bounds. This experience of God goes for the Abraham traditions: "God set Abraham on the way." It goes for the words in Exodus: "I will be for you the one I will be for you." It goes for the prophets' message of crisis and conversion, in which Israel was transformed into a landscape of the last days. It goes for Job and his cry: "How long?" Finally, it goes for early Jewish apocalypticism, which

32

reaches far into the New Testament, with its perception of history as a history of suffering.

Accordingly, this apocalyptic accent belongs to the history of Christianity's founding as well. What theology will later call "imminent expectation" spans the entire New Testament scene. After all, Jesus lived and suffered against its horizon. And Paul formulated his Christology in terms of its understanding of time. Pauline Christology is no ideology for the historical victor. Paul himself interspersed apocalyptic time elements in his Christology. One need only hear, "For if the dead are not raised, then Christ has not been raised" (1 Cor 15:16). There is no question that this way of thinking about time has to be recovered for contemporary talk about God and about God's Christ!

Of course, where will one end up with claims like these? It may very well be that they are apt enough for the biblical world. Yet does not a deep abyss separate us from that world? Are we not worlds away from Paul? Does not the attempt to remember biblical language about God and God's Christ in contemporary Christianity inevitably end up in a crude biblicism? Does not this sort of attempt betray a heavy dose of hermeneutical naïveté?

But let's see where hermeneutical naïveté is really at home! And let us be guided by the suspicion that in theology the appeal to hermeneutics can also serve to shut down the provocation offered by the biblical talk about God and to amicably relieve us of the burden of its "scandal." Some like to carry on this kind of hermeneutical rescue operation with the help of the so-called worldview thesis. One distinguishes between archaic and modern worldviews and then honestly and broad-mindedly consigns apocalypticism and theodicy, together with the way of perceiving the world connected with them, to the mythical worldview of archaic, biblical times. Yet is it not here that the real hermeneutical simple-mindedness rests? That is to say, the representatives of this kind of worldview thesis act as if, to begin with, there were a Christianity independent of worldview, historically and culturally naked, as it were, or a naked biblical idea of God, which one could then go on to drape with a great diversity of worldviews, indeed, worldviews that are mutually exclusive. But the imaginative perception of the world against the horizon of bounded time is nonnegotiable for the biblical idea of God![7] Or it is, unless one long ago betrayed it to a dualistic gnosis, with its axiom that time cannot be saved and salvation cannot be temporal, in order in this way to shield the Christian message of salvation from the abysses of the human histories of suffering and to spare it the apocalyptic disquiet of turning its question back to God.

Allow me in this context to pose a question that I find deeply troubling and that is directly connected with the contemporary relevance of the Gnostic temptation of Christianity that I was just talking about. Is it possible at all for us to connect our talk about God with the world's time anymore? Do we not subscribe to a secret dualism here? We cut our understanding of time completely in half, hand over the world's time to an empty, anonymous, evolutionary time, and try to bring just the time of the individual's life into some relationship with God. In so doing, however, have we not—in good Gnostic fashion—long ago abandoned the "creator of heaven and earth," and embraced only a redeemer God whom we think is to be found in the depths of our souls? Yet can a theology

---

7. The phrase "God crisis" describes not only a "crisis of faith," which for its part would only concern believers in their believing subjectivity. The "God crisis" concerns the world in its entirety, or the imaginative perception of the world as a whole, and is most closely connected to the problematization and upheaval of the heretofore regnant worldview. See in this regard my text "Gotteskrise: Versuch zur geistigen Situation der Zeit," in J. B. Metz et al., *Diagnosen zur Zeit* (Düsseldorf: Patmos, 1994), 76–92.

that holds to the profession of faith in creation escape once and for all the tension between the world's time and life's time?

To state the bare minimum: It is not the individual life world, but precisely the world of *the other* as well, not just the experience of the course leading ahead to one's own death, but also the experience of the other's death that sustains apocalyptic uneasiness. After all, the contents of the apocalyptic message—resurrection of the dead, last judgment—all take their bearings from the human history of suffering. The experience of crisis with which the message of the universal resurrection of the dead is connected is not simply the individual's experience of mortality but rather first and foremost the disturbing question of the salvation of the other from death—to be precise, those who suffer innocently and unjustly. This makes it the question of how justice is upheld for history's victims and vanquished, in whose debt we live and whose fate no struggle on the part of the living, however passionate it be, can change. In the apocalyptic traditions the hope for the resurrection of the dead expresses a longing for a universal justice that comes by virtue of God's power, a power that, in the apocalyptic vision, does not leave even the past alone. And the apocalyptic message about the last judgment affirms once again that before God not even the past is fixed. This message resists the way we usually reconcile ourselves to past suffering and forgetfully soothe ourselves in its regard. But what would happen if the day were to come when the only weapon people had to defend themselves from the world's misery was to forget about it? And what if they could build their own happiness only on the pitiless forgetfulness of the victims, on a culture of amnesia in which nothing but time heals all wounds? But then what would nourish resistance against the meaninglessness of suffering in the world? What would still inspire us to pay attention to others' suffering? What would still inspire a vision of a new, more comprehensive justice?

Johann Baptist Metz

Trial Runs for Today

How is this legacy of the biblical ways of speaking about God really doing in the Church? Does not apocalyptic literature provide a favorite source of quotes for fossilized traditionalists or narrow-minded fundamentalists? Would it not be better to steer clear of it, in favor of, say, a milder eschatology, more compatible with modernity? No. In my view the way one deals with this legacy continues to be the test of the authenticity and credibility of the Church's message during our times, and finally the test of theology's tenacity as well.

Over the course of the last several decades I have tried out ever-broader definitions in theological discourse for a Church that would not evade this challenge; some examples are the Church as "an institution of social-critical freedom," as "the bearer of a dangerous memory within modernization processes," as "a community of memory and narrative in discipleship of Jesus, who focused first on other people's suffering," and, thus, as a "Church of compassion." The last definition in particular makes it clear that the Church can only make its claims and appeals credible by continually uniting and holding together—in a way that is sensitive to theodicy—that to which fidelity to its apocalyptic inheritance compels it: the memory of God found in the remembrance of human beings' history of suffering.

The Church too is not above, but under, the authority of those who suffer, the ones whom Jesus made the criteria at the world's judgment in the parable of the last judgment in the "little apocalypse" of Matthew 25: "Whatever you have done or have failed to do to the least...." No discourse and no hermeneutics can get around obedience to this authority. Neither can it be enci-phered ecclesiologically. The criterion of this obedience can become practically *the* basis for a profound critique of the ways the Church conducts itself in the concrete. Has not the Church's proclamation too often forgotten that the way the Bible talks about God is spelled out in the remembrance of others' suffering, that the dogmatic memory of God cannot be broken free of the remembrance of suffering that cries out to heaven? Is the "God crisis" that stands in the background of the much-discussed church crisis these days not brought about in part by an ecclesial praxis in which God is (and has been) proclaimed with our backs turned to humanity's history of suffering? Does not the Church's appeal sometimes have such a fundamentalist sound to it because the authority of God that is being proclaimed has been separated too much from the authority of those who suffer? Are there not all too many examples of how little the Church lets the suffering of others touch it and its message: the cries of the poor? the cries of the victims of Auschwitz?

If the Church held itself accountable to the world by virtue of its fidelity to this legacy of its message about God, what sorts of things would it be compelled to do? Without any pretense of comprehensiveness I would name the following:

Sharpening a humane memory, inspired by the apocalyptic memory of suffering

The biblical tidings about God, as a message about bounded time, are expressed in a culture that is primarily oriented by memory, by the memory of humanity's history of suffering. As we have seen, the message about the death of God, as a message about a time without finale, expresses itself in a culture of forgetfulness, in forms of cultural amnesia. The eternity of time exacts forgetfulness as the condition of happiness. "Blessed are the forgetful" is the way Nietzsche put it, consciously echoing the biblical beatitude, "Blessed are those who mourn," those who refuse to reduce everything that has disappeared and passed irretrievably into the past to the level of existential meaninglessness, which is also to drive out any sense of what is missing from human beings' knowledge of themselves.[8]

It is true that remembrance of others' suffering is a fragile category in an age in which people think that ultimately there is no other way to steel themselves against the histories of suffering and atrocities that are continually breaking in on us than with the shield of amnesia. The day before yesterday it was Auschwitz; yesterday, Bosnia and Rwanda; today Kosovo. And tomorrow? Yet this forgetting does not come free. Has not Auschwitz greatly diminished the barriers to what is shameful between one person and another? Has it not done terrible damage to the bond of solidarity between all those with a human face? There is indeed not only a surface history of the human species, but a depth history, and the latter is absolutely vulnerable. Are not the present day orgies of violence and rape unconsciously attaining for us something of the normative power of "the real world"? Behind the shield of amnesia are they not undermining our basic trust in civilization, those moral and cultural reserves on which the humanity of human beings is based? Could it be that men and women have not only lost God under the spell of cultural amnesia, but are more and more losing themselves, losing in the process that which up until now we have so emphatically named as their "humanity"?

Promoting work for peace among human beings, based on apocalyptic traditions' sensitivity to suffering

Perceiving others' suffering and bearing it in mind when one acts is the unconditional presupposition for any really successful

---

8. Friedrich Nietzsche, *Beyond Good and Evil: Prelude to a Philosophy of the Future* (Cambridge: Cambridge University Press, 2002), 110.

politics of peace. For example, what would have happened in the former Yugoslavia if the peoples who lived there had acted according to the imperative of the apocalyptic *memoria passionis?* If, that is, in their conflicts they had remembered not only their own suffering, but also others' suffering, the suffering of their erstwhile enemies? What could have happened in the relationship between Israel and the Palestinians if the politics of peace there had continued to be guided by the axiom of the apocalyptic memory of suffering? What would it have meant for the civil wars in other areas of Europe if Christians had not again and again betrayed this apocalyptic *memoria passionis?* And only if a political culture grows up among us here in the European Union that is inspired by this sensitivity to suffering will the prospect grow as well that the Europe of the future will be a blossoming landscape, a landscape of peace, and not a landscape of imploding violence, not, that is, a landscape of escalating civil wars. Certainly one might ask how politically functional an inspiration of this sort really can be. The apocalyptic traditions I am appealing to here protest a pragmatism of democratic freedom that has cut itself free from the memory of suffering and has thus gone more and more morally blind. Ultimately political freedom cannot simply be about the relationship between one discourse partner and another, but rather—more fundamentally and entirely in line with the way that apocalypticism looks upon human history—about the relationship of one person to the endangered and overlooked other. Strictly symmetrical relationships of mutual recognition, as they are presumed in our discourse politics, finally never get beyond the logic of the laws of the market, of exchange and competition. Only by asymmetrical recognition relationships, only by one person turning to the threatened and victimized other, will the grip of the logic of the market be broken in politics. Not a few will think that this emphasis on asymmetry assumes an overly labored concept of politics. In fact, however, it only reclaims the inalienable relationship between politics and morality. For without this "moral implication," politics, global politics, would only be what we already see today: a hostage of the economy and of technology, with the so-called political restraints they lay down in this golden age of globalization.

Formulating a new relationship between the religions in the light of the apocalyptic memory of suffering, in the sense of an indirect ecumenism of religion: a common responsibility to the world in praxis

All of humanity's great religions are focused around a mysticism of suffering. This would also be the basis for the coalition of religions being sought here to save and promote social and political compassion in our world. This would happen in common resistance against the causes of unjust and innocent suffering in the world: against racism and xenophobia, against a religiosity that is nationalistically or ethnically impregnated, with its hankering after civil war. But it would also be in opposition to the cold alternative of a global society in which "man" is more and more swallowed up into economic and technological systems, devoid of human beings, with their culture and information industries, a society in which politics is in ever greater danger of losing its primacy to a global economy with laws of the market that long ago began abstracting from men and women in the concrete. This is where this indirect ecumenism of religions would be a political event, not for the sake of a pie-in-the-sky moralizing politics, not to mention a fundamentalist religious politics; but rather to support a global politics with a conscience.

What this requires of us is the theological honesty to pay attention to a serious question: How do two classical forms in religion of the mysticism of suffering deal with the suffering of others?

On the one hand we have the mysticism of suffering in the biblical-monotheistic traditions, with their apocalyptic background. On the other, we have the mysticisms of suffering from the Far East, especially in the Buddhist traditions, which are also winning more and more adherents in the West after the proclamation of the "death of God" and against the horizon of eternalized time, time without a finale. For in the end, Buddhism knows of nothing that corresponds even in a rough way to the thinking about the end times that has its roots in the Bible.[9]

The mysticism of the apocalyptically inspired traditions is at heart a mysticism of open eyes, a mysticism of an unconditional obligation to feel the suffering of others. Looking at Buddhism's foundational legends, it becomes clear that even the Buddha was changed by encountering others' suffering. Yet in the end he fled into the royal place of his interior, in order to find in a mysticism of closed eyes that landscape which is immune from all suffering and from the provocation of bounded time. In contrast to this, Jesus' mysticism is a "weak" mysticism. It cannot lift itself up out of the landscape of suffering; its mysticism ends up in an apocalyptic cry.

Consequences for Theology

When it comes to theology, the point would be to bring the *memoria passionis*, with its orientation toward the end times, into the logic of theology. I have tried again and again to point out that theology's most important task is to confront its Greek-Hellenistic inheritance with the ways the biblical traditions think about time—ways that are to a great extent metaphysically mute. I have discussed

---

9. See Aloysius Pieris, "Millenniarist Messianism in Buddhist History," in *Is the World Ending?* edited by Seán Freyne and Nicholas Lash, *Concilium* 1998/4 (London: SCM, 1998): 106–15.

this confrontation under the rubric of "anamnestic reason," a form of reason that forbids theology making itself into allegedly timeless, ultimate explanations, over and above historical remembrance.

With the form of reason that it developed and which is dominant today, the Enlightenment has a deeply rooted prejudice that it cannot overcome: the prejudice against memory. It calls for discourse and consensus and undervalues the intelligible power of memory, and thereby of anamnestic rationality. But what happens if reason continues to be determined by memory? Is there any way that a reason of this sort can be the organon of mutual understanding and peace? Does not praising reason in this way undermine a principal achievement of the political Enlightenment or recklessly abrogate it? Is it not historically and culturally rooted memories that stand in the way of mutual understanding and lead to continual and painful conflicts and dramatic demonizations of the other, which—at the end of this century—are feeding all the open or latent civil wars? The anamnestic reason we are seeking here wins its enlightened character and its legitimate universality when it knows itself to be guided by a specific memory, precisely by the memory of suffering: that is to say, not in the form of a self-referential memory of suffering (the root of all conflicts!), but in the form of a memory of others' suffering, in the form of a remembrance of the stranger's suffering. This *a priori* of suffering is what orients theology's claim to truth when, as a political theology, it incorporates the historical, social, and cultural situation in its talk about God.

From this I draw three extremely abbreviated consequences. *First,* with the Church and theology in view: Theology does not stand above or outside of the Church's memory, as a sort of objective observer. It gains its indispensable critical freedom in the community of the memory of the Church by continually examining the memory of God that is represented by the Church with regard to whether and to what degree it becomes the remembrance of the stranger's suffering, whether and to what degree the Church's dogmatic memory has separated itself from humanity's memory of suffering. And why in the future should not the university be the privileged place in which theology exercises this critical freedom, both in the interest of the Church and of society?

Second, considering the relationship between theology and the academic world *(Wissenschaftswelt):* The anamnestic reason that is indispensable to theology has as its goal the form of knowledge that is a sense of lack. When nothing is felt to be missing anymore in modern scientific knowledge, then talk about "man" becomes itself an anthropomorphism. That is, it is no longer "man" that is being thought of and intended, but nothing more than nature, that is, the human person as a being without memory, without subjecthood, a piece of nature undergoing an experiment that has not yet come to an end. Therefore, the way that theology knows, with its talent for memory, buttresses the elementary stubbornness of "the human" in the so-called human sciences, and belongs on their side, as long as the human sciences themselves have not been surrendered in an increasingly subjectless, technomorphic "systems language."

Finally: With the *a priori* of suffering that theology sets for reason, it also opposes the "profane" models and theories for social and cultural life. For example, it asks critically whether our posttraditional discourse societies that have cut themselves free from the *a priori* of the memory of suffering have really gotten beyond a logic of the market; whether, thus, they are guided any more by a vision of the responsibility of one person for another that is prior to any contractual or exchange relationship. With questions like these, theology is participating in the public debate, the interdisciplinary deliberation in the universities concerning the foundations of our common human life.

Johann Baptist Metz

The Alternative
(or, what are we afraid of?)

In conclusion let us take another look at Nietzsche. For him the time without finale, the time that the death of God unbounds, a time without beginning or end, is connected with the dawn of the great experiment that man himself has now become. He clothes this in the metaphor of "the open sea": "Finally our ships may set out again, set out to face any danger; every daring of the lover of knowledge is allowed again; the sea, *our sea*, lies open again; maybe there has never been such an 'open sea.'"[10] And in one of his most famous poems:

> There sat I, waiting, waiting—yet for naught,
> transcending good and evil, sometimes caught
> in light, sometimes caught in shadow, all game,
> all sea, all midday, all time without aim.[11]

The apocalyptic conscience, which has inscribed the sensitivity to suffering into its experience of time, highlights the deep ambivalence involved in the way we find ourselves in time. It calls to mind the sources of our anxiety. What are we afraid of? Archaic peoples were supposedly always filled with fear by the sense of the looming end of their lives and their world, and this mythical fear crippled their labors on their world. Something of this fear is evident as well in the contemporary fears of catastrophe. Yet in my view there is for contemporary men and women a fear that has

---

10. Friedrich Nietzsche, *The Gay Science, with a Prelude in German Rhymes and an Appendix of Songs,* edited by Bernard Williams and translated by Josefine Nauckhoff, poetry translated by Adrian Del Caro, Cambridge Texts in the History of Philosophy (Cambridge: Cambridge University Press, 2001), 199.

11. "Sils-Maria," in *The Gay Science,* 258.

become more radical. There is a fear not only that everything will come to an end, and that the planet could be destined for ruin; but there is also—more deeply rooted, the fear within all our particular fears, as it were—a fear that nothing at all comes to an end anymore, that there isn't an end at all, that one's individual end has no analogue, so to speak, in an end to the world. There is a fear that everything is being sucked up in the wake of a faceless, merciless time, which finally rolls over everything from behind like grains of sand in the sea. This dominion of time drives out every substantive expectation; it engenders that secret *anxiety over identity* that eats away at the souls of modern men and women. It can hardly be deciphered, since for some time it has been successfully practiced under the ciphers of experiment and progress, ere it is uncovered, very briefly, at the roots of our souls. So today there is a cult of unlimited experimentation. Everything is possible; anything can be created. Yes indeed. But there is also a new cult of fate. Anything can become obsolete. The will to experiment continues to be undercut by an unconfessed, unrecognized resignation.

An 1888 letter from Nietzsche to Franz Overbeck says: "I fear I'll be blasting the history of mankind into two halves."[12] According to this, the history of humanity to date would belong to one part, that part in which the apocalyptic message about time is still inscribed, inscribed, in fact, even where this message about time, in a secularizing inversion of its origin, has led to those power myths in our own century that tried to bring humanity's finale here by force. To the other part of history would belong, then, that coming humanity against the horizon of time without a finale: an innocent, wholly noonday humanity, forgetful of suffering; a humanity free of fear, a stranger to mourning. So, standing on the much-cited

---

12. *Nietzsche: A Self-Portrait from His Letters*, edited and translated by Peter Fuss and Henry Shapiro (Cambridge, MA: Harvard University Press, 1971), 126.

threshold of the new millennium, it seems to me that there is a singular and real alternative:

Either we slip away with Nietzsche into the mythical, Dionysian time without a finale, with our backs turned to the men and women of old Europe. This means being ready, with the "will," to see and accept time as the "eternity" really expected of us, as the *nunc stans* of a goalless time, beyond good and evil, beyond truth and falsehood, the landscape of "the open sea," that infinite experiment, without beginning or end, which humanity itself is within the eternal cycle of nature.

Or, we shift the threshold of humanity's future into a horizon—admittedly more dimly illuminated—of bounded time, time with a finale. The biblical-monotheistic early history of humanity's becoming human stands against this horizon too: setting out, exodus, holding one's head high in the awareness of the danger that it is quite possible for a person to lose his or her name, his or her face; the awareness as well that having a conscience is the reaction to being haunted by the stranger's suffering; the awareness that the human being exists as a subject who is unconditionally responsible and thus has the capacity for guilt, who becomes guilty above all of a lack respect for the stranger's suffering; the awareness too that the human being exists as a subject capable of the truth when and to the extent that he or she articulates this suffering of the stranger; the awareness, finally, that he or she exists as an obedient subject (for which on one point at least the "Thou shalt" comes before Nietzsche's "I will"), obedient, that is, to the irreducible authority of those who suffer, in which the authority of the apocalyptic God manifests itself for all men and women.

In my opinion the future of Christianity as we enter the next millennium rides on this alternative.

Joseph Cardinal Ratzinger, Johann Baptist Metz

God, Sin, and Suffering: A Conversation

Ratzinger:

Instead of figuring out just where I would disagree with Professor Metz in what he has just presented to us, it strikes me as easier to enumerate those points on which I agree with him....For instance, his appraisal of the hermeneutics that has tried to get free of the bite of the biblical message and to put it into a form that we can tolerate and, in contrast, the determination to grasp it in the ways that it gives offense....Or, his insistence on memory in the face of the contemporary culture of forgetting. And, as a consequence of that, the necessity to face the cry of the suffering—not to look in self-pity at ourselves, but rather to see the pressing reality of suffering and of injustice in this world. Then it will indeed be offensive to us that there is no justice, that it seems as if there is no God there. To this extent the question about others' suffering always turns into the God question....You have given us a great way of putting this with the phrase, "God crisis." We should not argue at this point over whether or not this is the best way of putting it. We all know what you mean.

Metz:

No, no! Perhaps you do, but…

Ratzinger:

Good, you'll explain it some more. I think I understand what you mean more or less. This, at any rate: That the God theme, in all its dimensions, in the claims it makes, in the challenges it levels, in its urgency, is the core; that all the other crises can be explained only in terms of it, and that we can only find an answer—if at all—when we start out anew from this point. Now it struck me, though, that the God theme was not really as present in the way you worked through your themes as I would have expected.

Metz:

I have used the phrase "God crisis" not to distance myself from the problems facing the Church but in order to draw attention to the fact that behind the Church crisis there is a crisis which is probably more profound and more radical. Now they say that a crisis for the Church is a crisis of faith….But if it is God that we are talking about, then it is never merely about the Church or about the faithful. Then it is about the whole world….And so it is always about God, even if the word is not always present….

You have commented on the context of the time theme and in so doing given a polemic against the concept of autonomy. I do this too; because of this we are not very reputable in certain areas of German theology. I wonder whether we have thought enough about the fact that we bear some responsibility for the way that modern freedom is interpreted as autonomy. Basically this is due to an insufficient way of dealing with the theodicy question and to the fact that we always take our starting point from Augustine's position (with which you are much more familiar than I), and think that the world's suffering really arose due to human guilt....Augustine said this—countering Marcion and Gnosticism—because he wanted to avoid any dualism in God. As a consequence, due to the exorbitant amount of suffering in the world, human sin has to take on enormous proportions. This is how a "hamartological"[1] overburdening of human beings arose, a kind of absolutism of sin, an over-moralizing of Christianity....

And if in modernity people wanted to express a notion of freedom in order to assert autonomy, and did it, then it was done, in my view, mostly in opposition to this absolutism of sin....That is also why neither modernity nor postmodernity will let themselves have anything to do with the history of salvation and the history of God anymore, which means that we theologians are faced with the challenge of studying the relationship between suffering and guilt afresh. Everything that I have learned about Jesus—not as an exegete but as a systematic theologian—comes down to this: Jesus' awareness of a person did not focus first on his or her sin, but on the suffering of the other....The theodicy question has to be strengthened in Christianity, even when it retains its aporetic character and freezes into the wordless cry of Job. In our times there are horrifically many cries rising up from humanity, outside of the Church too. Just as there are many prayers rising up from humanity, outside of the communities of faith too....People usually think that only believers pray and that prayer is one of the more intense forms of faith. How about if one gives up these notions and asks whether or not prayer could be more widespread than faith....To pray would mean:

---

1. *Hamartia*—the word used in the New Testament for "sin."

to ask God for God. Then I would ask who among us—yourself included, most reverend Cardinal—can hold himself or herself competent, whatever credentials he or she has, to say where a language of the children of men begins, and where a human speech leaves off, in which they ask God for God?...

Ratzinger:

You have covered a lot of ground, and have gone beyond theory to say something that moves our hearts….Jesus taught us not to be too modest in our prayers, not to pray for this or that. Rather, the gift of God we are to ask for in prayer is God Godself. With this we are once again up against the centrality of the God theme….

When it comes to the hamartological overburdening and the moral overtaxing of the Christian message, I would distinguish the two. I think that there really is a moral overtaxing of Christianity. This is precisely because the message about God, the testimony that God Godself is one who acts and not a mere "horizon," has gotten too weak. There is something of the deist hidden deep down in all of us: We no longer envision God as a subject who is really active in history—perhaps in the subjective, but even then in nothing but the subjective.

When this happens, when we finally stop assuming that God really enters into history and—all the laws of nature and everything we know and everything we can do notwithstanding—stop assuming that God is still the subject of history, acting in history; when we transform God into an indeterminate horizon, which somehow solemnly makes up the whole: then we are the only ones left to act. Then the entire burden of good and of evil rests exclusively on us. That is when moralism—the placement of moral demands on men and women—

takes on a form that cannot but overwhelm us, which we ascribe to God and against which we rebel. Shrinking from recognizing God Godself as active has led to this overburdening of men and women, the consequences of which we see all around us and sense daily in our efforts to be Christians.

This is why it seems so important to me to hear once again that God Godself addresses us and says: "Your sins are forgiven." To hear that there really is something that we call grace. And at this point there are good reasons for us to listen to Luther: Not only are there demands being made on me and my actions, and not only demands on humanity or any subject whatever; but rather, before anything else there is an action on God's part and it can transform me....

As I see it, we have to maintain that guilt arises from freedom...; that creation is stamped by the risk of freedom; that in the end we cannot understand God's logic, since sometimes it seems to us that the price has really gotten to be too high; but also that the reason for evil is to be found in human actions and the suffering becomes unbearable because it is connected with injustice, with the power of injustice. And so I think that in Augustine...somehow things really do balance out, that while it is true that he has put a heavy emphasis on the power of guilt, for him this really isn't the last word... since he turned the focus to Christ and knew that he not only looks upon our suffering but shares it, and that there is a power of God's which we cannot get a hold on, but which is real nonetheless. That is, there is a power of compassion that lets us live and lets us be of good cheer in life.

My question was this: You have spoken of being aware of others' suffering. With good reason...I am always moved by this wonderful saying of Origen's: God cannot suffer, but

God can suffer-with. Yet is it not also a part of the memory of suffering that we recognize the God who suffers-with: a God whom we cannot systematize but who nonetheless is moving us in the depths of our hearts? If it is only unresolved suffering that we perceive, then the only thing left is a cry of anger and despair in one's own existence. The only reason we can expose ourselves to being aware of suffering at all is that, in all suffering, one who suffers-with is present. If there weren't, then one would have to close his eyes, and in truth the only way left would be the way of the Buddha....We can keep our eyes open only because it is possible to be aware of God within suffering.

Metz:

I won't carry the theme of suffering over into God....My appeal is that we leave the mystery of suffering to human beings and that we not be too quick to concede it to God. Rather, we need to stay in prayerful strife with God, something which really cannot ever be superseded—being cognizant too of the forgiving God, of course. I absolutely will not cease to insist on the omnipotence of God, not in the sense of a stoic philosophy in which God remains apathetic about the history of suffering that human beings bear day in and day out. Understood in terms of the biblical traditions, God's power means that for God not even past suffering is fixed. What I have in mind is the connection with the hope in resurrection and the issue of judgment, which I have only touched upon with the greatest caution. But, I think that, over and against a pure idea of freedom, it plays a very important role—for sustaining the pathos for the justice of God and for avoiding surrendering ourselves either to the Marxist notions that you just mentioned, or the liberal ones.

I would like to say...that the theodicy question gives voice to the sense of grief over how little waiting and expectation, how little curiosity about what has not yet happened and not yet been said, lives on in Christianity: curiosity about God combined with a conviction that it would in any case be an assault on God Godself were theology to try to find a formula that would justify God in the face of human suffering and possibly even to state this formula as a doctrine. For if there is a justification of God, then it is that God will justify Godself, in God's own time. This is what really the whole of the biblical tradition teaches us.

Jürgen Moltmann

From the Beginning
of Time in God's Presence

For the Truth of Theology in Freedom

In 1967 Johann Baptist Metz gave us the phrase "the new
political theology." Many have followed him with their own
thoughts on this; others "saw a conflict emerging that could go
deep indeed."[1] According to Metz, political theology was supposed
to be "a theology with its face turned to the world," and "a way of
talking about God in these times," and thus it had nothing at all to
do with the feared "politicization of theology." It took its origins
neither from political Catholicism nor from a "Marxist Messianism."
What it did do, however, was to understand theology's political
mandate, in addition to its ecclesial one. If the Church is the "messianic people" of the coming Kingdom of God,[2] then not only can
theology be a "function of the Church," but it must (like the Church
itself) become a function of the Kingdom of God in the world. It
has then its own proper responsibility in the community of the
Church, a responsibility which no one can relieve it of and which
the Church must respect for the sake of the coming Kingdom.

---

1. Joseph Ratzinger, *Milestones: Memoirs, 1927–1977*, translated by Erasmo Leiva-
Merikakis (San Francisco: Ignatius Press, 1998), 135.
2. Vatican II, *Dogmatic Constitution on the Church (Lumen Gentium)*, chapter 2.

Political theology's forum is the public sphere of a given society. It gets involved in the *res publica* in the name of God's justice (Barmen Declaration, thesis 5). This happens in public talk about God, lamentation to God, hope in God. As a consequence it belongs in the intellectual public sphere of the university too, in the form of Catholic and Protestant faculties of theology. The community of the Church remains its subject, the Kingdom of God its project, the citizenry its context, and the spiritual situation of the age its *kairos*.

It is unjust to accuse theology in the state universities of being "state theology," intending thereby to exclude theological faculties from the universities and to ecclesialize theology, so that all that is left in the universities is a neutral science of religion. In democracies the state universities guarantee theology "freedom of research and teaching." When the Nazis destroyed this freedom in the German universities, it was a good thing to found ecclesial colleges, since in dictatorships like this the churches could end up being the last free spaces for truth. But today this free space for truth is threatened from another direction. Since the fall of socialist dictatorships and ideologies in Eastern Europe, the special theological institutes from Tartu to Bucharest have returned to the universities as theological faculties. In Western Europe, however, atheists and fundamentalists, lay persons and parts of the Catholic hierarchy, are pressing for the secularization of the universities and the ecclesialization of theology, following the French, Spanish, and Italian models. This would, however, be "the end of time" for any public or political theology. But political theology, despite the fallibility that it shares with all theologies, does not deserve this.

From time to time there are conflicts of conscience in theological faculties between the ecclesial and academic mandates of theology. "Freedom of research and teaching" serves the knowledge and dissemination of truth, in this case of theological truth. Only "the truth shall make you free" (John 8:32) and preserve your freedom. Ecclesial directives, fidelity oaths, and instructions, such as the 1998 *motu proprio "Ad tuendem fidem,"* are not necessary for baptized Christians. But if one thinks that they are necessary, they should be directed to persons' free consent on the basis of their own persuasive force and not to a forced consent on the basis of threatened "penalties" or a threatened withdrawal of one's *missio canonica.* According to a collective Christian conviction about the universal priesthood of all the faithful (men and women), there is also a common office of theologian and a magisterium of the Church to which all are accountable: "We are the Church!" Theology and the Church live halfheartedly when women are excluded from office. Thus, it can only be the collective responsibility of all believers, bishops, and theologians "to preserve" the faith, if indeed it is the faith that needs our protection and not the other way around.

Here on this earth, faith needs the free space of trust. It only lives in a kind of "domination-free communication." It flourishes in consensus; in compulsion it withers. Talk about God that is censored is no true talk about God and cannot keep talk about God from going wrong either. To name names: Controversial theologians such as Rudolf Bultmann, Hans Küng, Leonardo Boff, and many others are still in the council and community of theologians, in which it is truth that is at stake, even if the Church has limited their freedom. The Church cannot on behalf of God give the truth less freedom than "the world" does, but must give it more freedom.

The Modern Time Crunch

"When two people say the same thing, one of them is unnecessary" (Russian proverb). I will take my starting point from a somewhat different analysis of time than Johann Baptist Metz's. It is not the "time that runs endlessly onward" of biological evolution and of human progress that fascinates men and women even today and makes them blind to threats and apathetic about catastrophes. It is the *loss of a sense of confidence in time.* Nobody knows whether or not he or she has a future. Nobody knows if it is a sudden nuclear end or a slow ecological end that awaits us. The half-life of the nuclear waste here in Ahaus is so unimaginably long that nobody can keep track of it anyway.

Twenty years ago we still worried about the future. Today, besides the "pop apocalypticism" of the year 2000, expectations about the future, both good and bad, are getting scarce. Only the present is left. "THE FUTURE IS NOW" says the computer ad, promising to fulfill the age-old human desire to be simultaneously present to all places and all times. We overcome expanses of space and time with bullet trains and the Concorde, with e-mail, cell phones, fax machines, the Internet, TV, and videos, and the virtual world of cyberspace. This seems to have become the new God-complex of modern men and women: I will become omnipresent to all places and contemporaneous with all times. If this is possible, then the future won't matter to me and I will forget the past.

Every available fact and datum about the past is recorded in a data bank or on the Internet. Anyone can call them up at any time and make them present. Space abolishes time. For example, in Bonn the *Haus der Geschichte* [House of History] has been made out of the open, unconcluded processes of German history. There, all those things that earlier occurred in sequence are present at the same time. Our old villages become "museum villages." Historical exhibits offer us "a day in the life of Stone Age man" or "face to face with the Middle Ages": folklore for tourists. The living past is transferred from temporal memory to the omnipresent gaze. We put an end to history's time by "museumizing" it. Facts are rendered into dramatizations and dramatizations into data banks of the present. Computers and the Internet also make the future present. What was once unknown, surprising, and therefore dangerous in history's time, and was thus a future that one had to risk, is carried over into possibilities of this present, which can be evaluated by computer simulations. Those future times that we have to wait for become presently calculable possibilities. This is how the present takes command of the future.

In the year 2000 we will be able to experience the great boom that this God-complex is having most dramatically in the Millennium Dome in London. There one will be able to wander through all the ages of humanity, from "Lucy" to Einstein, and play out in computer circuitry every possible future for humanity, desired or undesired. One will also be able to see through the "giant man" from the inside: his muscles and nerves and his computer brain. There is nothing modern that won't be there. Disneyland will pale in comparison, like an old fashioned county fair. If you don't want to go to London, you can have a similar experience at the EXPO 2000 in Hannover. We will feel like gods at these global exhibits: present everywhere and "everywhen" at the same time.

But our life's time is still bounded time, finite, brief, and fleeting. How can we exhaust the fullness of modern possibilities in the world? The answer is simple: Speed up the tempo, presto, live faster. "Stay in the fast lane; don't let anything get away." Being everywhere "up to date" and present, and absorbing everything that can be seen on videos or slides: This is when you are in all things and all things are in you.

But what about death? What about when it comes and says to us, "Your time has run out"—it is the end of your time? No problem here either: Die quickly and painlessly. Thanks to medicine, the "sudden death," so feared in the Middle Ages, has become our friend. And after that? Still no problem. Anonymous burial has become the ritual of disappearing for our times. In Hamburg they make up 25 percent of all burials; in East Berlin, 50 percent; in Chemnitz, 75 percent. "And his place knows him no more" (Ps 103:16).

The Fullness of Time

The provocation of talking about God arises not from fitting in but from standing out. That is why I am counterposing the Christian experience of God with the dream of being simultaneously present to all times. The Gospel "is a message about time" (Metz). For that reason I will not develop the Christian experience of presence speculatively or mystically, but rather I will read it from Christ's experience of time.

1."When the fullness of time had come, God sent his Son...." (Gal 4:4), and "the time came for her to deliver her child" (Luke 2:6). According to this, time is "fulfilled" in the coming of Christ into this world. Which time? Whose time? For the political theologians of Constantine's court, such as Eusebius of Caesaria, it was the time of the Roman Empire, which reached its apex under Augustine. When this Caesar brought peace to the world (*Pax Romana*), God sent the savior into the world (*Pax Christi*). From this providential concatenation of earthly and heavenly monarchies follows the *Imperium sacrum*, which, according to Dan 7, is "the fifth monarchy," the reign of the Son of Man and the saints of the most high, consummating the world's history and putting an end to its time. But since, after all, "the savior" of the peoples wasn't born as a Roman in Rome, but as a Jew in Bethlehem, what we are really talking about here is the fulfillment of Israel's time. The time of waiting for the fulfillment of God's covenant promises has come to an end;

Israel's "night (under God's hidden face) is far gone; the day (with God's shining face) is near," as Paul puts it in Romans 13:12 in his announcement about time. In "the fullness of time" this past comes to an end and a qualitatively new future begins: out of distance from God comes closeness to God; from a painful "sense of God's absence" (Metz) comes the experience of the all-embracing, enlivening presence of God's Spirit (Ps 139). In "sending his son," as Paul puts it, God Godself comes into time. In God's Christ-Shekhina the eternal one "dwells" in our midst; in God's Spirit, God "dwells" in our mortal bodies. Time is determined by what happens in it. Everything has its time. How is time determined by the presence and indwelling of God in it?

2. After the Baptist was imprisoned Jesus came to Galilee and announced: "The time is fulfilled and the Kingdom of God has come near" (Mark 1:15). This is the *messianic announcement about time:* The promised time is here. "Today" this scripture—that is, Isaiah's prophecy of the Messiah and of the messianic Sabbath (Isa 61:1–2)—has been "fulfilled" in your hearing, proclaimed Jesus (Luke 4:18–21). "Today" salvation has come to this house, he said to the chief tax collector, Zacchaeus, not without adding, "for the Son of Man has come to seek out and save the lost" (Luke 19:10). Truly, "today" you will be with me in paradise, he said to the man crucified with him (Luke 23:43). The coming of God's reigning presence "fulfills" time. There can be no compromises when it comes to the "today," and no relativizations by any sort of proviso ("but not yet"). This presence of God is undivided and indivisible. It is no expectation, not even an "imminent expectation," but a real presence.

3. We find the same "today" in the apostolic proclamation of the Gospel. The present is the *kairos of salvation.* "Now is the acceptable time," says Paul (1 Cor 6:2), repeating what Jesus announced in Nazareth about "the time of God's favor" (Luke 4:16ff). The time

of the messianic Sabbath is also announced in the apostolic Gospel. "Today is the day of salvation." The chronological course of time, for which all times are equivalent, comes to an end with this kairological understanding of time. Everything has its time, and the present belongs to salvation.

4. Standing between the kairos of Jesus' proclamation of the Kingdom and the kairos of the apostolic proclamation of Christ, there lie the depth structures of the apocalyptic and eschatological experience of time. On the one hand, we have "The hour has come; the Son of Man is betrayed into the hands of sinners [the pagan Romans]" (Mark 14:41). "Night is coming, when no one can work" (John 9:4). We hear Jesus' complaint: "Could you not stay awake with me one hour?" (Matt 26:40). While earlier it was "the day" of salvation that was spoken of, now we hear only about "an hour." Yet in this hour of absolute abandonment no one can stay awake. We don't have "open eyes" to endure "the averted face of God," and to stay awake for God in that absence of God in which everything sinks into nothingness. But Jesus "stays awake" for this in Gethsemane, in this "hour," and he cries out on the cross. In this hour of God's darkness it is not only a time or his time that comes to an end, but the world's time, every time. That is why the conjoined states of his abandonment in Gethsemane and Golgotha are apocalyptically colored. If time in general comes to an end, then the world comes to an end too, the *cum tempore* was created and *sine tempore* forgotten.

On the other hand, it is impossible to picture that "eschatological moment" of the resurrection of the dead-and-abandoned Jesus into "the life of the world to come." For neither do we have eyes for this "moment." No one saw that process itself, but the risen one "let himself be seen." It was Paul who used the image of "the

61

moment" for this. "Suddenly, in a moment, at the sounding of the last trumpet" (1 Cor 15:52), the dead will be raised up and changed.

This "eschatological moment" is not identical with the "kairos of salvation" in time, but rather it is the end of time in the beginning of eternity. It was Kierkegaard's and Bultmann's mistake to confuse these two and to make the present in time into the "atom of eternity." The "eschatological moment" is the moment in which transitory time (*chrónos*) is changed into eternal time (*aevum*); out of moral life comes eternal life, and out of temporal creation comes the new creation. The distinctively Christian brings eschatology into apocalyptic: in the end—new beginning.

God's Presence in the Modern Time Crunch

Becoming present to all times and places is a quantitative expansion of the present into the past and into the future. The translation of the past into data banks in the present represses history's unfinished processes. The translation of the open future into present possibilities drives the surprising and the new out of the future. As with every repression, these repressions of history come from fear and a widespread blindness concerning what is other and strange.

1. The first impact of God's presence in the kairos of the present can be seen in the reduction of the human present to a human scale. In this experience of God, as Luther said, true men and women are formed out of "unhappy and arrogant gods," since in the God opposing us—*the God who is here*—we perceive our limits. We are not wrenched out of space and time, becoming infinite, but rather we come back to our own space and our own time and become finite. In God's presence we experience the end of our past and the beginning of our future. The talk about God that is pro-

voked by the modern "end of time" is *talk about God for the opening up of our times.*

2. The kairos of salvation can only be salvific if it brings the power to *heal memories*, both personally and collectively. Its redisclosure of history clears the "house of history" and grasps history in the unfinished, unexpiated, and unreconciled processes of the past. Nothing "passes away with time." Everything that was is present at the depth levels of memory, giving to us and making demands of us: the histories that went wrong, the wasted opportunities, the missed possibilities. When the archives are opened, the events are revisited and the poor judgments are audited.

But there are also the hopes of past generations, which form the backdrop against which their descendants appear. There is so much future in the past that will not let the past be past. The experience of the presence of the *God, who is here,* sets us on "the search for times past" in the *God who was there.*[3] God's presence in the horrors of the past heals our painful memories and dissolves the repressions by means of which we hold them at arm's length. With the modern "end of history," our talk about God is provoked to *open up past history.*

3. If we can once again allow there to be memories of the past, then we will also connect them once again with our hopes for the future. Without memory there is no hope; without hope, no memory. The past and the future are interwoven historically. The talk about God that is provoked by the modern "end of the future" (in the slogan: "The future is now") opens up a new horizon of the future, for it talks about the *God who is coming here.* In God's future, perspectives open up for a definitive justice, in which human his-

---

3. [The allusion is to Marcel Proust's work, *Le recherche du temps perdu,* whose German translation is *Auf der Suche nach der verlorenen Zeit* ("searching for past/lost times"). The English translation is entitled *Remembrance of Times Past*—trans.]

tory's victims and perpetrators are brought together. Perspectives open up on the new creation of all those things that have been irrevocably destroyed here. A future is awaited that goes beyond personal death, a future that does not make us vanish into anonymity. The talk about God that is provoked by our modern anxiety about time creates *a sense of confidence in time.*

4. Last but not least, the presence of God's Spirit in time awakens in us *the virtue of serenity.* We will become immune to the growing and artificially inflamed fever over the millennium. The year 2000 is no triumph; neither is it an abyss opening up at our feet. It would be better for us to get ready for "the day after." Whoever is certain of the presence of eternity has a lot of time. We must not live in a bigger rush in order to have more of life; on the contrary, we should live more slowly in order to experience life more deeply. Only the one who eats and drinks slowly eats and drinks with satisfaction. In God's presence we too become wholly present and experience the moment with undreamt-of intensity. The young Bloch once called "the opacity of the lived moment" "the opacity of the lived God." God already "dwells" in time. Every Sabbath, every Sunday, and every felt Kairos leads into the presence of the eternal, which leaves us time.

Eveline Goodman-Thau

Writing History as a Messianic Hermeneutics

It is a part of Judaism's paradoxical character to live out of the conflict of having its home within time and also in eternity, in the here and now and in the transcendent. The foundation for this experience, which has been a formative one from the earliest beginnings right up to the present day, lies in the religious-ethical drama of Judaism, in which God alone is the creator of the heavens and the earth from nothing and the one who guarantees the existence of the world through his revelation. In place of the mystery of the cosmos, human beings come to the fore, each one individually and humanity as a whole, as the bearer of the idea of God. The power of the ethos is entrusted to human beings and the moral drama, the doing of the ethos, becomes the center of his or her life. The creation of the world, what God has in mind for the world, finds its expression in human beings, and in this way the word of God is made a reality.

A God of History

From now on, the fate of the world is bound up with God's fate. The conflict between being and nonbeing is settled once and for all, and the human world order established. Nature and humanity thus acquire a temporal dimension within which the idea of history is born. Messianism in its entirety, as the prophets teach it, is only the development of this orientation of our being, defined by God and made manifest in time. In this respect the God of Israel really is a God of history. What Judaism represents and has communicated to the nations is the idea of a historical process that is sustained by justice and by an ethos. There always has to be a span of time that stretches between promise and redemption; life has to be engendered and shaped; history, finally, has to be cultivated. But at some point that great hour will strike when, as in the beginning, eternity will break into time and the immanent and the transcendent will be united.

So, in contrast to other peoples, the Jewish people are not familiar with the writing of history in the classical sense. It is not the facts of history that were important to it but rather the way and the form in which a person recalls his or her history—the point at which biography and history intersect. In this process the person as a remembering individual is one link in the chain of collective memory. The memory of the departure from Egypt, the fact of God's intervention in Israel's history, becomes the cipher for Jewish memory, in which remembered history leads to redemption. The redemption from the house of slavery in Egypt is an anticipation of the definitive redemption at the end of time.

From forgetting—memory's converse—comes terror, the fear of alienation from God, and looming catastrophe. "Take care that you do not forget the LORD your God, by failing to keep his commandments, his ordinances, and his statutes....Do not exalt yourself, forgetting the LORD your God, who brought you out of the land of Egypt, out of the house of slavery....If you do forget the LORD your God and follow other gods..., I solemnly warn you today that you shall surely perish (Deut 8:11–19).

In the recapitulation of the encounters with God in the wandering in the desert, the revelation on Mount Sinai, and the entry into the promised land, we find a basic pattern for the passing on of tradition as it has become Torah (teaching), in the biblical canon, and in its elaboration in Midrash and Talmud.[1] In the Bible, God's encounter with God's people is narrated in the form of a history, which certainly has a beginning but no end. The five books of Moses begin, "In the beginning God created the heavens and the earth," and they end with the words

> Never since has there arisen a prophet like Moses, whom the Lord knew face to face. He was unequaled for all the signs and wonders that the Lord sent him to perform in the land of Egypt, against the Pharaoh and all his servants and his entire land, and for all the mighty deeds and all the terrifying displays of power that Moses performed in the sight of all Israel. (Deut 34:10–12)

The Messianic Tradition

Here beginning and end do not mean a purely temporal dimension, but rather an event: the encounter of God with the man Moses, in a "face to face knowing." The time and the geographical site of Egypt are only significant and are only visible, so to speak, because it was there that God knew Moses and worked all the signs and wonders before his people, "before their eyes." It was not just the Jewish people who witnessed this, but rather "Pharoah and all his servants and his entire land." And it is precisely this witness that

---

1. Like other religious traditions, the Jewish tradition is based on a written canon that both contains the history of the people of Israel and forms the foundation for the Jewish faith.

opens up the possibility of interpretation. What we are dealing with here then is not an end, but rather an opening, a beginning: The signs must be interpreted.

The final prophet in the Jewish Bible is the prophet Malachi. But this end doesn't represent a conclusion either, but rather a message of hope for the future. It closes with the words,

> "Remember the teachings of my servant Moses, the statutes and ordinances that I commanded him at Horeb for all of Israel. Lo, I will send you the prophet Elijah before the great and terrible day of the LORD comes. He will turn the hearts of parents to their children and the hearts of children to their parents, so that I will not come and strike the land with a curse." (Mal 3:22–24)[2]

The message of the last prophet appeals to that of the first. Malachi (my angel) speaks to his people together with Moses (the one drawn out of the water, the first-sent of God), and admonishes them to be ready for the last day. However, it is not only a matter of turning back to God, that is, of keeping his commandments, thus keeping the past in mind. It is also a matter of "the hearts of the parents turning to their children and the hearts of the children to their parents." This means building a bridge between the beginning and the end. In short, it means establishing a messianic tradition in the religious sense. Only when the generations have a mutually renewing and fructifying effect on each other does God's word pass down through the ages and lead to redemption. It is only then that the parents and the children become God's witnesses. Thus it is not just a matter of the reconciliation of the parents with the children but

---

2. [This corresponds to Mal 4:4–5 in the versification of the Christian canon— *trans.*]

of the possibility of renewal and change that historical time leverages open for a messianic future.

The biblical writing of history, as the spring of remembering, is also the foundation of a messianic hermeneutics in interpretation. The Talmud stresses that the Prophet Elijah will come in order to unite traditions from various epochs.

> R. Joshua said: I have received as a tradition from Rabban Joḥanan b. Zakkai, who heard from his teacher, and his teacher from his teacher, as a *Halakhah* given to Moses from Sinai, that Elijah will not come to declare unclean or clean, to remove afar or to bring nigh, but to remove afar those [families] that were brought nigh by violence and to bring nigh those [families] that were moved afar by violence....And the Sages say: Neither to remove afar nor to bring nigh, but to make peace in the world as it is written, *Behold I will send you Elijah the prophet...and he shall turn the heart of the fathers to the children and the heart of the children to their fathers.* Rabbi Simeon says: in order to bring agreement where there is matter for dispute.[3]

---

3. Mishna Eduyoth 8.7. According to this text, then, preparing for the coming of the Messiah does not mean canceling the law, but rather a process of emendation within the tradition so as to take into consideration opinions that have been either adopted or excluded by a majority decision. The arguments of the rabbis over the interpretation of Scripture are brought to an end with the insight that all opinions are "words of the living God," in order to make peace between parents and children. [This translation is taken from *The Mishnah*, translated from the Hebrew, with Introduction and brief explanatory notes, by Herbert Danby (Oxford: Oxford University Press, 1933), 436f. It should be noted that Goodman-Thau rearranges the order of the passage. In the original, "Rabbi Simeon says..." is placed immediately prior to "And the Sages say...."—*trans.*]

Eveline Goodman-Thau

Eternity in Time

History, as the foundational messianic experience recalled to memory, finds its deepest expression in Jewish prayer, where the studied text from the Torah becomes the prayed text. Jewish liturgy is entirely constructed on the basis of the content and language of the Bible and is taken to be oral teaching. In the ancient Jewish morning prayer it says: "Day by day and eternally God in his goodness renews the work of creation." Just as God continually renews his creation, so every day the human being recognizes anew his or her covenant with God. God is not only the creator of the world, God has bound Godself in revelation and each day effects a New Creation. This is how remembered history becomes in the Jewish tradition a prayer for redemption.

The entire history of the people of Israel is lived anew in every age, winning thereby its symbolic significance for the future. Everything that happens offers the opportunity to explore and express in intelligible, unequivocal language what was learned in faith in order to shape the future. When the normal course of history is interrupted, as, for instance, in the destruction of the Second Temple, then the Jews internalize this and mold the symbols that make up the cornerstone for what is to come. In this sense we think back on the famous saying of Rabbi Elazar and Rabbi Chanina: "Read not 'your children' (*banayikh*), but 'your builders' (*bonayikh*)."[4]

The crisis of tradition is thus fruitful grounds for a new beginning. Every hour, every situation, is a time for decision.[5] Religious

4. Babylonian Talmud, Berakhot 64a. From *Berakhot,* translated with notes, glossary, and indices by Maurice Simon (London: Soncino Press, 1990).

5. *"Hakkol safuy wehareshut netuna"* is the way the rabbis named the paradox between God's omniscience concerning the future and the free choice of human decisions within time. ["All is foreseen, but freedom of choice is given." Aboth 3:16, from *The Mishnah,* 452—trans.]

determinism (God's omniscience) requires human freedom (the decision). The messianic hermeneutics as a writing of history in Jewish tradition lives off this tension. The openness of interpretation on the textual level opens time up for eternity. This is how a dynamic hermeneutics between revelation and tradition came into being: Revelation as written teachings finds its actualization in tradition, in the oral teachings as the expression of the interpretation of revelation within historical time.

In this respect every interpretation of scripture is an inbreaking of eternity into time, a present, which breaks time open messianically and opens it up for redemption. A rabbinic saying expresses this quite succinctly: "Whoever makes an interpretation in the name of its author brings redemption for the world."[6] Conservative, restorative, and utopian forces were able to exist side by side and even enrich one another. As soon as the present no longer promised to be the place, goal, or realm of messianic hope, then these expectations were projected onto an ideal past or a utopian future. It was thus less a conflict between conservative, restorative, or utopian forces as it was the question of a felt tension in the present between a redeemed and an unredeemed world, in which today is lived on the one hand as the day between yesterday and tomorrow, and, on the other, is experienced as a gateway for the Messiah: a tension between *lived* time and *experienced* time.

At the end of his 1925 essay on "The New Thinking," the philosopher Franz Rosenzweig wrote on the character of his new epistemology, which he compared to the philosophy influenced by the ancient Greeks: "The concept of the verification of truth

---

6. [See Aboth 6:6, *The Mishnah*, 460. There the saying is translated: "[H]e that reports a thing in the name of him that said it brings deliverance unto the world." [Here Goodman-Thau uses the German "Auslegung" ("interpretation") to render the Hebrew *dabar* (utterance, something said)—*trans.*]

becomes the basic concept for this new epistemology, which takes the place of the old epistemology's noncontradictoriness-theory and object-theory, and introduces, instead of the old static concept of objectivity, a dynamic concept."[7] He called his new way of thinking a "messianic epistemology, which ranks truths according to the price of their verification and the bond which they found among men."[8] This perspective engenders an understanding of time that, at the end of the second millennium of the Christian reckoning of time, can lead to a new meeting of Christianity with Judaism.

Religion and Modernity

There is no doubt that the Jewish apocalypticism of late rabbinic Judaism forms the spiritual background for the emergence of Christianity and the messianic new beginning for the first Christians. However, we Christians and Jews cannot overlook the difference in the history of the reception of these events. The inbreaking of eternity into time means in the Christian world the introduction of a new calendar, so that one now speaks of "before" and "after."[9]

In my opinion this difference plays an important role for the theme of religion and modernity, the question, that is, of how one can live as a Jew in a secularized world. In this regard there is no surfeit of attempts in the conversation between philosophy and reli-

---

7. Franz Rosenzweig, "The New Thinking," in *Philosophical and Theological Writings*, translated and edited, with notes and commentary, by Paul W. Franks and Michael L. Morgan (Indianapolis, IN: Hackett Press, 2000), 109–40, here 135.

8. Ibid., 136.

9. This fact really becomes clear to a Jew when dates according to both calendars are used in Israel for all official (not just religious) institutions and documents. The year 1998/99 is from Rosh Hashanah on the year 5759. In Jewish terms, we are thus in the sixth millennium.

gion to try to mediate reason and faith. While this is not the place to pursue these attempts further, it is, however, worthwhile thinking about what it means to live in an age in which the human being seems to have become the measure of all things. Does this mean being lord over good and evil? Or does it not rather mean taking on responsibility for our respective traditions, which govern the ways that religion and ethics encounter one another in the action of each individual? The biblical word for this action is ḥesed: an active love that has to continually orient the freely acting individual. This love may neither be derived nor deduced from the law, but rather requires the free decision of the person. This freedom elevates the human act to a higher level, so that the covenant—philosophically, the relationship to the absolute—is ratified and secured anew.

The question of the outcome of human action, the question of redemption, if you will, is always an open question. But one should also not avoid this question, which recalls the well-known saying of Rabbi Tarfon, from the "sayings of the fathers": "It is not thy part to finish the task, yet thou art not free to desist from it."[10] By his or her action a person corresponds to the promise of God, to build an *olam chessed*, a world of active love, as it says in Psalm 89:2, in which every standard of good and evil is to be found.

It is the integration of men and women into this relationship with God that gives them the confidence to choose the good and to give meaning to the time that they live in this world. The yoke of the law is thus the key to freedom, and the idea of the covenant is continually connected with the possibility of release—in the sense of a loosing of the covenant from its historical fetters. This liberation is tantamount to a *reversal of time*. It no longer flows from the past into the future; rather, it is stayed by the inbreaking of "the now" and

---

10. [Aboth 2:16, *The Mishnah*, 449—trans.]

of "the event" into time. It is the "today" of the present reader (as a messianic hermeneuten) that redeems the text from time and in this way creates a place where human lives, embedded in time, receive a significance that extends beyond time into eternity.

The great attempt in the history of the human spirit to bind the radical separation of good and evil to the absolute is doomed to failure. Western thought's enduring dualism gives an only apparent relief to human beings at the price of surrendering their most primordial freedom.

Ethics and Religion

The God of Israel is a guardian of rights and of justice, a judge of all the earth. And what of the election of Israel: of this small, insignificant nomad people, who have survived in spite of all its persecutions and expulsions, despite the monstrous events of the past century in this country, a people who have survived without a language and without a country right up to the present day? In this election Israel has a security that consists not only in the protection of its God, but is also based on the protection of rights and the overcoming of injustice. This is something that is not already embodied in an absolute heavenly community, nor in a treaty, a constitution, or an *ekklesia*. Rather, it has to be realized here, on earth, in human doing and acting: that is, in time.

This is perhaps the God of Israel's greatest gift: that God teaches men and women what is right and just, as it says in the morning prayer before the "Shema":

You have loved us with a great love, God, our God, you have given us a great and overabundant gift, our father, our king, for the sake of our fathers who trusted in you and whom you have taught the law of life. So grant us and teach us, our father, merciful one, and have mercy on us and give us the ability to grasp and understand in love the breadth of your teachings, to hear them and learn them, to guard them, to do them and to preserve them....

God's love for human beings consists of this: that God does not keep God's teachings locked up in heaven but has shared them with men and women. It was certainly not the cosmic order that was the decisive thing; rather, the God of heaven and earth taught the men and women formed by his own hands how to distinguish good from evil. That is why Judaism doesn't hear the Garden of Eden story saying anything about an original sin (the word sin occurs only in Gen 4, with the fratricide). Rather, for Judaism the story tells of the gift of free will, of the knowledge of good and evil, and of death.[11] This gift of God to men and women is no command; it is the path to holiness (Lev 19). The people are not commanded to become a good people, but a holy people. Every ethical demand consists of the elevation of human beings to the level at which the ethical merges into the religious, at which the ethical, in its difference from the religious, "is suspended in the breathing space of the divine," as Martin Buber said.[12]

---

11. In connection with this there is a brilliant interpretation of the medieval exegete, Rashi, who explains that, before they had eaten from the tree of knowledge, Adam and Eve could certainly have named the world (*logos*), but they would have been value-free names, and thus valueless—precisely because they did not know the difference between good and evil.

12. Martin Buber, *The Eclipse of God: Studies in the Relation Between Religion and Philosophy* (New York: Harper Torchbooks, 1952), 104. Israel is supposed to become holy, for God is holy. "The imitation of God by man, the 'following in His way,' can be fulfilled naturally only in those divine attributes turned towards the human ethos, in justice and love, and all the attributes are transparent into the Holiness above the attributes, to be reproduced in the radically different human dimension. The absolute norm is given to show the way that leads before the face of the Absolute" (105).

The presupposition, however, for connecting the ethical and the religious in this way is the insight that in being created by God the human person is posited by God in *freedom*, and that the person can stand only before God in this independence. This is where the dialogue between God and the person begins; the person is fully aware of his or her existence in complete freedom and simplicity, and constitutes him or herself as such before God, as an individual, becoming God's partner in time.

And how should we envision this more specifically? After creation is completed, the garden planted, the tree of life and the tree of the knowledge of good and evil in their places, we read, "It is not good that the man should be alone" (Gen 2:18). This is a central theme in the creation story, the negative analogue to God's repeated statement: "It is good...." What we have here is an inner dialogue of God's about the existence of the human person who represents the temporal dimension within the natural world: time as a caesura, so to speak, between the person and the world, which can only be adjudicated by the person as a temporal being in distinguishing between "good" and "not-good."

Creation is only completed when the man has a counterpart. The true naming of the world consists in a decision for the good and for the not-good. "I will make him a counterpart," an *'ezer kenegdo*, a helper over against him (Gen 2:18).[13] "A helper" and "over against him." It is not only the man and the woman who stand in this paradoxical relationship, but the human person and God.[14] Adam's (man's) temporal dimension is thus initiated by a further creation: the creation of the woman. Everything is finished; everything

---

13. [The German here is "ein Hilfe ihm entgegen," which is an alternative translation to the usual German translation (and most English translations) of *'ezer kenegdo* in Genesis 2:18—*trans.*]

14. "'Ezer" is a word that the Bible also uses for God.

is already created masculine and feminine, yet the biology of the human race is incomplete without that intervention of God's that gives the woman to the man Adam as the condition of his own independence—a part of him, but only now visible as a medium of knowledge: not as knowledge of absolute truth, but as an insight into the independence of the person to choose good or evil. The man only knows himself as a man when God gives him the woman as his counterpart and in this divine counterpart gives him his independence. The man and the woman, called from now on *Isch* and *Ischa*, are partners in God's creation, which they take care of and maintain, in good times and bad.

God had not planted the tree of the knowledge of good and evil in the garden in order to teach man absolute truth, but rather to teach them freedom of choice, the decision for the good, without which creation cannot continue to exist. The Torah, as the tree of life, as instructing us how to live, is still the guarantee of an unbroken bond between God and humanity. It is still the affirmation of God's trust in human beings, a covenant in which the truth is forever taken up. Thus, every hour continues to be an hour for real decision—until the Messiah comes.

Joseph Cardinal Ratzinger, Johann Baptist Metz, Jürgen Moltmann, Eveline Goodman-Thau

---

The Provocation of Talking about God: A Discussion

Moderated by Robert Leicht

Leicht:

> Let me ask for two points of clarification from this morning's session: Johann Baptist Metz spoke of talk about God. May I as a Protestant ask: Are *we* the subject of memory, or is it *God?*
>
> And—provocatively—is not the concept of the new political theology really a big mistake? For, as I understand you, Herr Metz, you certainly want a *theological* theology. And this is what bothers me a bit. First of all, since this theological theology results (correctly) in a certain distance with regard to particular political options…, then theological theology does not necessarily mean ecclesial theology because—to the disappointment of many of your friends—it does not engender any

polemics in the realm of ecclesial politics. Doesn't this make political theology conceptually confused?

Political Theology

Metz:

First of all, on the public character of theology, which Jürgen Moltmann has also addressed. I think that the public gesturing of theology that I have in mind with political theology belongs to the fundamental mission of the Church. What I mean is that there is a form of identity that the Church is compelled to take on not just because of its message alone but also due to the urgent situation in which we are living today. Limiting this public articulation of the Church or doing away with it altogether would not be doing the Church any favor. That is why I am absolutely of the opinion that political theology is not a misunderstanding, but rather a pleonasm. If it were possible to do theology differently than as political theology, then of course I would do a different theology.

So when I use the word "political," the last thing I am thinking about is party politics. As far as the reformed tradition, which I value very highly, I would say that since we (Catholic Christians) do not want to let reason be absorbed by faith or let nature disappear, as it were, into grace, and since as a consequence we cannot change politics into the certainty of faith either, this is precisely why there has to be a political theology. What happens with reason, what transpires in that sphere that we call nature, and what plays out in the realm of politics, all of this, at least according to the Catholic tradition, can be dangerous for its own identity. That is why one has to argue with reason, with the philosophers, since they are absolutely a part of determining what is Christian....

Needless to say, we are not beholden to a particular philosophy, nor are we limited to a particular understanding of nature, nor, of course, to a particular politics. But we know that from these realms, in particular, possibilities and challenges can arise concerning that which we understand under the category "Christian." There is no such thing as a "pure" Christianity. Rather, Christians are placed right in the middle of the contested territory between nature and grace, reason and faith, and also in the struggle between politics and salvation. That is why we simply cannot walk away from the table satisfied, as if faith were no longer at stake....

The First Vatican Council still knew that God is first of all a theme concerning humankind or a theme for reason...that as the creator of all things God can be known with certainty from the created world, which is an outrageous thing to say. In the Second Vatican Council, on the other hand, the talk was only of the God proclaimed by the Church, and that outrageous claim was in general not risked anymore. Therefore, in the name of a Catholic sense for the tradition, I am making suit for this vision and this task, which certainly also touches on the point that Jürgen Moltmann was making when he spoke about the university as the place established for reason's discourse. Theologians are in a certain sense the agents to reason authorized by the Church. I would hold that removing them from this fray, as it were, and from this place would be a kind of assault on the self-definition of the faith. Note, after all, that the First Vatican Council's declaration on the natural knowledge of God was not just one view among others, but a defined dogma....

The First Vatican Council is still vulnerably exposed to my question about whether or not there has been for some time now a God crisis, whereas the most recent Council, by simply speaking only of God within the confines of the Church, already represents an immunization to this crisis. And, with all due respect for his theology, Karl Barth advocates the thesis "God comes from God" (the human person is no longer in the middle) as a theological trope for immunizing us, so to speak, against the God crisis. The person, with his or her immense doubts, seems to have no competence for God in the sense intended by the "natural knowledge of God." This would be something like the direction that my answer to you would have to take if I had enough time.

Autonomy in Critique

Leicht:

Some people were amused or astonished this morning, Herr Metz, when you asserted that you were in agreement with the cardinal in rejecting a focus on autonomy. I heard a few people say, "That's what I always thought." Therefore, I have a question now for the cardinal. Is it legitimate, from your perspective, to distinguish between a person's wish not to be the slave of another, on the one hand, from the insight that a person cannot be God's master, on the other? And if this distinction is legitimate, under what conditions must a Christian think of him- or herself as another Christian's superior?

Ratzinger:

I have spoken only of man's self-emancipation from God, and have really only touched on the theme of autonomy in this sense...that God, in a completely understandable logic of

existence, appears in his infinitude to be a threat to our finitude, and that for this reason men and women want to be free
of God in order to be free themselves....Over and against this
image I have tried only to suggest that in reality our relationship to God is not one of dependency, but is the condition,
the possibility, of our freedom. Only when the love that
grounds us opens up the space for our existence can we really
be free and really be ourselves.

The Second Vatican Council has very explicitly emphasized different kinds of autonomy: the autonomy of politics
with respect to the hierarchy, the autonomy of scientific
authorities versus nonscientific ones, and so on. These are
autonomies that have inherent relativities...to the extent that
the autonomy of politics simply cannot mean that it is free
with respect to claims made by the good and by the truth, and
that there cannot be other authorities that, to be sure, do not
command anything, but do have something to say to politics
which is said with great seriousness. If it were to be ignored,
this would be a distortion of the autonomy of this realm itself.
There is then no doubt that there is something at issue here:
that there are real autonomies, and that we had to learn this
in the course of modernity....

I think that your question about whether a Christian can
be a superior to another one is a simplistic one. Of course he
can. You know this yourself, don't you? Mind you, being a
superior means enjoining on everyone a common obligation
to a higher obedience, and it does not mean making oneself a
burden on someone else, but rather, discerning a particular
function in a common service to some cause. And there is no
doubt that this is the case in the Church too, and not just in
the Catholic Church, although the problem of ecclesial

authority was worked out differently in Protestant Christianity....With this in mind, what I would say, let's keep our feet on the ground.

Metz:

I am for a Church from the ground up—in this case. (Laughter.)[1]

Consensus, Truth, Freedom

Leicht:

A while ago Jürgen Moltmann made a remark concerning the object of this little disagreement. He said that truth flourishes in consensus. I find this astonishing. So many times I have had the experience that error flourishes in consensus, and that the truth comes out only when there is disagreement. How then does truth flourish in consensus?

Moltmann:

Well, truth certainly can fare poorly in disagreement, for what side is it supposed to be on, Herr Leicht, on the one side or on the other? Whereas with consensus one can be confident of arriving at a common view. I have nothing against disciplinary procedures in matters of doctrine. But this has to be discussed in fraternal conversation, and one must strive for community for as long as possible. Every Church structure and office has to be embedded in the community of the

---

1. [Ratzinger ends with a common German saying, "Lassen wir die Kirche im Dorf." Literally translated it means, "Let's leave the church in the village," but it can be used in any situation where someone wants to urge his hearers not to get too wrapped up in abstractions or theoretical constructions, but wants to stay "in the real world." Metz replies, "Ich bin für die Dorfkirche," which means, "I am for the village (or local) church." He turns around the aphorism in order to voice his advocacy—not unlike liberation theologians—of a "base" church. Hence the laughter from the audience–*trans.*]

Church. The Church community has to support the pastors; the Church community must support the bishops, and the converse. So, we need to strengthen these presbyteral and synodal elements in the Church, even when it comes to as difficult a question as whether someone is still a Catholic theologian or whether the Gospel is being proclaimed or not....Freedom is integral to the truth; and the community, in which people deal with one another in mutual trust, is integral to freedom. This is what I said.

But may I take this opportunity to say something more to my friend Metz? He is certainly a good Catholic theologian but he doesn't understand anything about Protestantism! (Laughter.) He thinks that Protestants are all fideists, when in fact all the great philosophers of modernity—Lessing, Kant, Fichte, Hegel, and so on—were Protestant philosophers. And Metz's "friend" Nietzsche was the son of a Protestant pastor. So we don't have to catch up when it comes to this issue— nature and grace, or faith and reason.

Metz:

And so this means we have to fight it out with Kant, Nietzsche, and the rest as your proxies, so to speak, since we are the ones who represent the principle of reason in theology! (Laughter.)

Moltmann:

In place of that, we'll carry on the struggle against Aristotle for you!...What I wanted to say is this: Don't you think that since *Gaudium et Spes* the old schema of nature and grace has been replaced by the scheme of history and eschatology? Now we are to read the "signs of the times," which is precisely what is going on in liberation theology too..., a theology that is certainly responding to Metz's concern that "natural theology" be thought of as something that has to do with theology as a whole, as something that concerns everyone.

Leicht:

So it sometimes seems to me, my dear Johann Baptist Metz, that your anti-Protestant polemics is only supposed to hide how Protestant your thought is.

Metz:

But I haven't done this for a long time!

God Talk in an Unredeemed World

Leicht:

Frau Goodman-Thau, a question for you: We have heard today that one of the paradigms in Johann Baptist Metz's thought is remembering others' suffering. This is certainly significant for the contemporary German scene, insofar as the advocate of a particular memorial in Berlin is always cryptically stating that "Redemption lies in memory." You have put it with greater precision today. You said, "Remembered history becomes prayer for redemption." I certainly do not understand this to mean that the culprit would only have to remember his or her deeds and then be redeemed. I would like to have a better idea of what it was you were wanting to remember. What is remembered? One's own guilt or the promise that God has given to God's people?

Goodman-Thau:

When Catholics and Protestants have difficulties with one another, how can we then have a conversation with Judaism? That is my question, which admittedly I cannot answer with an offhand remark to the effect that the only difference between

Judaism and Christianity consists in what one does in the interim time.

I was a little disturbed about the question that you, Herr Metz, asked in view of the stranger's suffering: "How can I share in the suffering of the other?" Judaism...asks: "Why does it go so badly for the world's just, while the evil do so well? Is this kind of world just?" If one transfers these questions once again into a political theology (and I am really in favor of that, not that one theologizes politics, but that one politicizes theology, since, as the prophets have already taught us, there is only *political* theology), then the Jewish answer would go like this: "You suffer from the world not because you are guilty, not because you worry about great theological or philosophical questions, but because there is injustice of which you are not personally guilty."

The suffering each one of us endures over his or her own sins is, as I see it, already the greatest penalty. Even the criminal suffers under the weight of his own sins, which does not mean that his or her sin is forgiven, but *does* mean that he suffers when he does evil....The question is this: "How do we go on living in these times?...How do we go on living as survivors?" For indeed, all of us in this generation, in this century, whether Jews or Christians, are all survivors of the Shoah. I wonder why it is that in the Christian sphere it is always a matter of whether one was guilty or not. This just isn't the question! The question is this: "How do we deal with the fact that *others* were guilty?" This is my question; this is why I take part in Jewish-Christian dialogue; this is why I talk with Germans....

This, as I see it, is what it means to suffer the stranger's pain: that we become guilty if we do not take it upon ourselves. It is a messianic moment, a martyrdom, when one takes on another's suffering, establishes peace, and structures one's life accordingly. This is "my" memorial. To add on the names of the victims would be obscene. For within every name of the victim, a name of the perpetrator is inscribed. One ought to build a memorial where only the names of the perpetrators are listed....

There is a long discussion in the Talmud about when the Messiah will come, and if in this it is a matter of works or of redemption. In the end the debate is settled with a saying: "The Messiah comes for those who are in mourning." Do we mourn? How do we mourn? How do we live in an unredeemed world? This is a central question for Jews and Christians alike, especially in view of the issues of autonomy and of suffering. I have to make a decision here and now, on my own. Is this an issue for me or not? This goes for all of us.

Morality and Obedience

Leicht:

We should now let the public have a word....

Große-Rüschkamp:

My question is for Cardinal Ratzinger. Herr Metz has emphasized in his lecture that the authority of the suffering and of the oppressed are constitutive for theology. Latin American liberation theology has demanded the political implementation of this authority of the suffering. If it is true that there was a surprisingly broad consensus here this morning, then I cannot understand why you do not now rehabilitate the liberation theology that you condemned in the eighties.

Kerstiens:

I am a parish priest in the Ruhr Region, one of Johann Baptist Metz's first doctoral students. I was able to follow much of went on this morning quite well. Despite this I became very uneasy, since what was said to me too far removed from the people that I deal with. Everyone was agreed that it was a matter of a sensitivity to the suffering of others. I would like to name this suffering in the concrete: a sensitivity in the Church's leadership for impoverished pregnant women. Thank God that the German bishops are still showing a little backbone, but what is coming here from faraway Rome is lacking in [another sensitivity too]: a sensitivity for divorced people who remarry...who want to make a new beginning in faith. I myself supported the *Kirchenvolksbegehren* in our city, where homosexuals have told the story of their history of suffering in the Church.[2] We must be so close to men and women that we not only speak of solidarity with and sensitivity to those who suffer, but also name them by name, even the ones who suffer from the Church. I think, for instance, of many women who are offended by the reasons given for why they cannot be ordained to the priesthood....

I cannot picture a God who has a sensitivity for lay people as a God who insists first and foremost on the rights of the clergy. I cannot imagine God as a God who denies the Eucharist to a base community somewhere deep in the jungle,...even though there are men and women there who are experienced, capable, and accepted enough to celebrate the liturgy with their communities....Sensitivity to the suffering

---

2. [The *"Kirchenvolksbegehren"* is a critical lay movement, which started in Austria in 1995 and spread to Germany (and beyond). Conceived as a referendum movement, it collected signatures calling for fundamental changes in church politics and structure (e.g., more lay participation and consultation in church government, opening the deaconate to women, the rejection of obligatory celibacy for priests, and more liberal doctrines concerning human sexuality). Not unlike "Call to Action" and "Voice of the Faithful" in the U.S., the movement has taken on a more organized form *("Wir sind Kirche")* calling for radical reform in a number of areas. See their website at http://www.we-are-church.org/de/—*trans.*]

of men and women—including those who suffer in and from the Church—demands a closeness to these people, and it is this closeness that I find missing.

Leicht:

This had to be said. The applause underscores how important it is that this be discussed....First I would like to call on Herr Metz.

Metz:

I would like first to say something about the Church from which people suffer (this is all very difficult, I admit). Without this Church, without this memory of two thousand years, burdened by dark but also liberating experiences, we would probably not be talking about God or theology at all anymore. This means that first of all I concede this to the Church. This sphere, within which we talk about God and about salvation, is not something we can take or leave as we please. The second thing I would like to say is that in this Church there are things that are beyond discourse, dialogue, and the possibility of doing it this way or that. There is thus an obedience in this Church that is prior to dialogue, understanding, disagreement, and consensus.

This can be seen in the most important parables that Jesus told us, with which he made a place for himself narratively in humanity's memory. In the parable of the Good Samaritan, for example, he depicted a situation in which it is not possible for one to think things through—Do I have to do this or that? Can I ascertain where the meaningful action lies? Rather, it is a situation in which one has to obey. Here I can only stand by the one who is lying on the side of the road, fallen into the hands of robbers. When I say God in the sense intended by Jesus and by his parables, then when I am faced with the affliction of others, I have to be ready to revise the notions I have held up until now. This is a fundamental imperative, which makes it clear that there is a nonnegotiable obedience in the sphere of the Church that tells these stories. I have called it obedience to the authority of those who suffer. These are the two background assertions that are extraordinarily important to me and that I would like to integrate into the sensitivity of the life of the Church.

Now then there is, if you will, still another level on which this obedience has everything to do with human morality. For morality isn't justified by consensus either. If there is then something like an unconditional claim on us, then naturally it exists before I have agreed on it with others, or it exists even if we don't. And now the catalogue of opinions of the Church's tradition enters in, in which these moral ideas, which have an impact both on individual life and on interpersonal relations, play a role. For example, the question of marriage, of homosexuality, the ones that were just listed.

One can object that I have not sufficiently treated questions like these in detail. All the same, I do try to take up these questions in my theological work, and to continually emphasize the human history of suffering as the criterion for the norms of ethical and religious behavior that the Church proclaims. I mean this in the sense of the biblical dowry of "compassion," which I hold to be the most precious dowry of the biblical traditions for European culture—alongside the Greek dowry of "theoretical curiosity," which has helped us to develop the modern scientific world, and the Roman dowry of being able to grasp what justice and institutions mean for our common life.

Take the question of the remarriage of the divorced. It touches on a fundamental institution of the Church. For example, I have tried to pose the question to the Church of what it really wants to do with its sacrament of penance. We have the impartial statement of the president of the German Bishops' Conference that in Germany private confession is "clinically dead"....Nonetheless the Church has had and continues to have the tremendous responsibility of being mindful of this sacrament. Would it not then be possible to come up with an ecclesial form of penance, in which, for example, the question of a painfully failed marriage could be treated differently than it is with the familiar examination of conscience? The question, thus, of whether there could not be a sacrament of penance in which, in certain cases and under particular circumstances, there might be the possibility of admitting the divorced to the sacraments?

All of these questions involve one having patience: not just patience, but certainly patience too, when dealing with the Church's "elephant's memory," a memory that is salvific, since we can only still talk about religion in a substantive sense at all because of its lasting guarantee.

Leicht:

You will understand why I have listened patiently here. The reason why a Protestant should only intervene very carefully, in as difficult a dialogue as this, is that he thinks it more respectful to labor away at such questions than to take them lightly. I would like to summarize the questions to Cardinal Ratzinger in the following way: Is it possible for you to imagine that one might talk about a Church that people suffer from, and at the same time hold on to the image of a non-sinful Church that as a consequence cannot say "mea culpa"?

Ratzinger:

At some point I would also like to say something about the question of theology in the university that Herr Moltmann posed and Herr Metz underscored.

Leicht:

We should give priority to the question from the public and then move on right away to this one.

Paths to Freedom

Ratzinger:

On the first question, I regret that people in Germany still refuse to take note of what particular branches of liberation theology said and what they did not say, and that people assume that a critique of one strand of this theology was at the same time a "no" to struggling on the oppressed's behalf and constituted taking the part of the oppressor. I can only ask here that, for a start, people get beyond the "political correctness" that openly forbids one from thinking differently, and that they get a feel for the texts themselves....The promise that the new world will arise and injustice disappear through a sudden change in political government is simply a false promise. Political processes do not take place according to a monolithic dogmatism that only permits one point of view and that passes things off as scientific that are absolutely not scientific. They require freedom of discussion and patience....I would also insist quite emphatically that the relevant texts from the Church's magisterium have never taken a position against the legitimate desire for a path to freedom and for a society worthy of human beings, for overcoming misery. Due to his origins the pope has a passion about this that nobody in the curia could gainsay, even if he were to want to.

On Mr. Kerstien's question, I would make a very similar observation. Namely, you assume—and this makes me angry—that with all of these difficult questions there is only one permissible point of view. If you are saying that those involved in pregnancy counseling who think it is right for things to be balanced out between the Church and the state have no sensitivity when it comes to women's suffering, then I say to you that this is not true....That there is only one way for this and only one allowable opinion—we have to reject this. It is a dictatorship of thought against which I will vigorously defend myself....

The problem of divorced people who remarry is no doubt one that deeply distresses all of us, and is one for which no one has a final answer. For we certainly have to defend the good of the indissolubility of marriage, this good of the Church, this sacrament which the Lord has given us. That is why we cannot think that the quick solutions are really the better thing for men and women....For inner events like these, a break in something that is supposed to be definitive, the disintegration of a love, the collapse of a community with children, who now are the ones who suffer—all of this is certainly not solved by manipulating the Church's law. I don't want to downplay the problem; but what I really want to say is that it is a very complex issue, and, as I see it, all the churches have to suffer from it, and none of them, I think, could say that they have a solution that is completely correct. Orthodoxy's approach, to take an example, is a respectable one, but it has been very tightly linked with civil law, and the grounds for separation have become so broad that at some point the character of indissolubility in the bond disappears....

With the issue of the readiness to marry and, thereby, the actual constitution of the definitive bond of marriage, the Roman Catholic Church has tried to find a way to connect indissolubility—which is not something within the Church's discretion but is a point at which the Church itself is bound to obedience—with human frailty. I can say that those of us who belong to the relevant authorities in Rome are really always struggling and asking what the pope can do and what he cannot do. And then there is this strange reversal: people who are really rather opposed to the papacy say, "He can do this if he only wanted to. The Church can do this." And those who are rather favorable to the papacy say, "No. The primacy is an obedient office. The pope absolutely cannot...."

There remains a part of suffering that we cannot solve by institutional means. And this is where I would like to bring in something that is really fundamental....I can remember a debate that went on in a Catholic university. One of the cardinals who was present impressed me by saying, "It is very important to help people learn how to suffer and to recognize what is positive in suffering. For whoever does not learn how to suffer will not be able to live either. There is no such thing as a life without suffering."...One of those who was also taking part, a physicist, reacted very harshly: "One must not learn how to suffer. You have to fight it." Haughty words, I would say. Naturally medicine (and the other sciences) should do what is in their power to help prevent unnecessary suffering. But there is no life without suffering, and suffering is also, I think, a gift that God gives us, which helps us become human and without which love cannot exist. I think that it is one of the lofty educational missions of the Church to be present in suffering and to make God's pity, Christ's pity, present in such a way that suffering becomes meaningful. Naturally this does not mean that we may cause suffering, but surely there are limits, at which point we cannot prevent suffering and must help to bring about the redemption of suffering from within.

Suffering from the Church

Ratzinger [continuing]:

This brings me to Mr. Leicht's question. I think that people also suffer from the Church, and for a great variety of reasons....The question of the sense in which it is possible to talk about a sinful Church is currently occupying Catholic theology....Especially among medieval theologians there was a critique of the hierarchy of a sharpness that not even the boldest adversary of the hierarchy would permit him or herself today. [Read] texts of Albert the Great or Bonaventure, breaking upon the mitered heads of Europe and using a very powerful terminology....Or think of the visions of Hildegard of Bingen: a Church of great beauty, but with clothing that is appallingly stained and torn.

I simply cannot venture a conclusive answer here. But I do think that there really is an innermost inviolability to the Church, which doesn't mean the purity of the prelates, but rather this: In the final analysis there is a core of holiness in the community of Christ and the saints, to which we can cling and from which we ourselves receive holiness in turn. The Church is not totally polluted. I am always moved by the prayer that the priest says in the Roman Liturgy before communion, at that dramatic moment at which I have the audacity to receive the Body of the Lord: "Look not upon my sins, but on the faith of your Church." Look away from my sins, or else I would have to perish or flee. It doesn't say, "Look instead on the holiness of the Church"; rather, "on the faith of the Church." The Church continues in its innermost core to be the faithful, the locus of faith, the guarantee of faith, if you will, with its "elephant's memory" that Metz just spoke about....

There are further contested questions..., but it seems to me that they get us into the classic arguments, in which it would simply have to be asked once again: "What does the Church believe? Where is the Church bound by obedience and where is it free? Where is it unable to prevent suffering, but must give aid in the midst of suffering?" To work all this out on a case-by-case basis here, would, I think, take us beyond the task that I have undertaken for today.

The Social Location of Theology

Ratzinger [continuing]:

The first thing I would like to say about theology and the university is that I am not aware of any political campaign by the Vatican against theological faculties in state universities. On the contrary, I would rule this out, although it is not directly a part of my responsibility. Theological faculties are currently being established one by one in the state universities of Poland. What one does find, on the other hand—not in the Church but among people who live in the Church and outside it—is a dispute over the degree to which it is society that makes this assignment. Herr Metz has said that the university is the place that society sets up for theology to carry out its public responsibility and to argue with reason and about reason. It just has to be asked here: Is society in fact setting this place up this way anymore? For surely there are massive social changes on the horizon....

At any rate, I would contest the claim that it is only in a public institution that theology can attend to its public mandate, which it certainly possesses (on this there was for me never any doubt, and cannot be any doubt, as well, once one has grasped the nature of theology). Indeed, this legal structure only exists in a very specific part of the world, that is, only in those places where there were still national churches after the Enlightenment. This means, then, Central Europe, Scandinavia, and Great Britain, and nowhere else in the world: not in the Romance nations, because they carried out the separation between church and state in a very different way; not in North America, because there churches took a congregational form from the very start and in general are not a part of the national sector. No one can say that theology is not attending to its public responsibility in these places....

And finally: It surely cannot be the case that the Church is not capable as a Church of creating a free space within which real theology can be carried on with the freedom and accountability that are proper to it. That one absolutely needs the vehicle of the state to do this would really represent a deficit in the Church, which I cannot accept at all, since we certainly know of counterexamples in this instance too. Naturally there are also always examples of narrowness, handicaps, and negativity. But these are also certainly there in the theological faculties....This is not a plea for the abolition of the faculties in state universities. I belong to a relatively small group of people on the contemporary theological scene in

Germany who not only spent his entire studies, but virtually his whole life, in national faculties, and who would really find it painful if something like them didn't exist anymore....But what I would like to see is a free and open, critical yet also respectful, debate about what all of this should look like in the future of our country.

Leicht:

Ladies and gentlemen, time has not stood still for us. We have come to the end, so to speak. I have to ask pardon of all those people who had hoped to say something and now will be disappointed. But I think that what was discussed was also very much of interest even for those who were not able to speak. To conclude, I would like one more time to ask the Jubilarian: When and where do we hear God's talk?

Metz:

Talk *about* God, which has certainly led to theology being formed in a specific way, which, once again, has to do with the universalism of the message that theology is supposed to represent—as Christian it is no longer bound to one people only. It is now intended for humanity as a whole, and it must now talk to all men and women about this God before it can make it clear that it originally stems itself from talking *with* God. This means that this talk about God has to understand itself as a reflexive form of a totally different form of talk, one that we call the language of prayer....It seems quite important to me that theology too never forgets that it is an *actus secundus*, thus a second act, which presupposes religion and prayer, or even the Church too. Or presupposes hope, and this a hope that is—this would be my final word—always so great, so tremendous, so extreme, that it can never be hoped for oneself alone....Much more could be said on this. But, allow me to stop here.

Leicht:

Today, yes, my dear Johann Baptist Metz, but not in the years to come! All the best!

Jürgen Werbick

Epilogue:
What Is It Time For?

For faith and theology, taking one's bearings on the end of time signifies anything but being able to adopt a stance "outside of time." Rather, it demands of them a nuanced awareness of the times (and perhaps liberates them for it too); it requires the most focused awareness possible of what it is time for. God's benevolent will (to put it theologically) desires and ought to take place in terms of what it is time for. Theology's dilemma—also the one faced by the community of all those who are seeking a path through time in the footsteps of Christ, the crucified one (1 Pet 2:21)—is that there are passionate arguments in the Church and in theology over what precisely it is time for. Needless to say, these arguments can spring from the temptation to get out of one's obedience to what is, after all, in its central features really the clear challenge that comes with being a Christian. This was discussed this afternoon. Perhaps too these arguments show a refusal to endure the necessary *noncontemporaneity* of the Gospel. But surely what is mostly at issue here is whether and where the "scandal" is due to the noncontemporaneity of the Gospel, or to a scandalous insensitivity and hard-heartedness when it comes to the challenge of our *own* time. Finally, what is at issue is whence and to what end authentic discipleship has to allow itself to be challenged.

An awareness of the times in the Church will also always mean an awareness of differences. The "veil of ignorance"—about where the *next step* goes that one has to identify *now* as the necessary one—cannot be lifted or penetrated by X-ray vision by the experts or officials, however competent they be. It continually requires the prophetically ventured, and thus also contested and thoroughly fallible, faith-hypothesis about what it is time for, what the next steps are, which one would finally just have to risk, a hypothesis concerning how to keep faith, today and tomorrow, with the one who "opened" this path and made it "passable," the one who, when it comes to what is most decisive, is himself the way.

An awareness of the times means an awareness of the path through time and in it, however, also an awareness of the risk that one must take in walking that path, seen, of course, from the vantage of the final goal that is disclosed in faith. Fidelity to the sources has to be concretized in *the risk of the present moment;* and to refuse being a part of one's times, and to desire, either in a naive way or with sublime reflections, to stick only to what is beyond time, is to refuse that risk.

The risk of being a part of one's times is substantial, particularly from a theological perspective. Whoever takes that risk honestly will know how quickly one, becoming caught up in the present, becomes a slave to the times, is taken in by "what everybody knows these days," and then just misses or rejects what it is time for. Taking an orientation on the end of time, if it does not remain all too abstract, can break the dictatorship of "today" and free us from the chains of what "still works" today. It can validate anew things that have been forgotten or repressed, things that it is time for us to appreciate today and that would open up the future to us. That said, however, refusing to be a part of one's own time is an evasion; perhaps it is even an attempt to will oneself out of time so that doubt in the face of the uncertain path that lies before us might be left behind in favor of confidence in an infallible wisdom and those who administer it.

Theology can and must work together with others, so that people do not enter into the venture of being a part of their times in a panicky, unfeeling, or forgetful way, which, however, would also mean without hope. It can and should (here in Germany) cooperate in the social "laboratory" where this venture is mapped out (and certainly not just scientifically and technologically) and then critically accompanied: the university. Theology has introduced the curiosity of faith into the common questioning and research of the *Universitas litteratum;* the curiosity that is provoked by men and women's religious questions, provoked in particular by the biblical traditions and inspired by the Gospel of Jesus Christ; a curiosity about what is still to come, since God is still entering into this world and transforming it by God's Spirit; a curiosity about how that reality that Goodman-Thau named today as the distinctive feature of messianic time could be—that nothing or nobody is excluded violently, and nothing or nobody is received violently. This is why it is virtually impossible for us theologians to understand it when this cooperative work comes under ever-greater suspicion within the Church and in specific cases is even blocked—this too was discussed today. It is certainly clear that there are certain sociopolitical interests that are pushing for a decision to exclude theology from the university. With no little consternation, we wonder whether there are interests and options within the institutional Church that are suggesting a coalition with these sociopolitical forces.

I have spoken of the risk of being a part of one's times, of the high risk of error that no science can escape. If the sciences were to desire infallibility, they would lose their capacity to learn in the process. To learn also means essentially this: to draw the appropriate conclusions from mistakes and errors and to work one's way with good grace out of false alternatives that misrepresent the problem at hand. Theologically it means *conversion* in those places where one has gotten stuck. Is one allowed to think it a theological possibility (and make an issue of it in a solidaristic critique as the situation requires) that in the praxis of the magisterium there can be a too-precipitous recourse to infallibility and definitiveness, which threatens to cut short the requisite learning process?

Theology lives with the risk of fallibility in the public spheres of the university and society, as well as of the Church. Thus, it must always allow errors, alleged or actual, to be pointed out to it—by the Church's magisterium, for instance. However, does this justify the simple, sweeping claim that the hierarchical magisterium is always on the safe side of an issue, so to speak, and that in every respect it has a sounder grip on the criteria that put it in a position to point out to theology its "lack" of fidelity to the sources? Is there not also a "lack" of the will to endure the uncertainties, experiences, needs, hopes, and suffering that come with being a part of one's times, and a "surfeit" of the will to stand above all of this and make definitive statements? May one not wish of the teaching office of the shepherds a somewhat greater solidarity with those who day in and day out have to live with the risk of trial and error, the risk of disgrace, so to speak, but who also choose to live with this, since they know that otherwise there are many things that we will never learn?

What we want is that in the Church too there be trustful conversation and responsible argument about what it is time for, and about what inevitably gets overlooked if one simply reacts with fear to this. And we would like to think that this conversation is even meaningful and possible in those places where there might first be grounds to demand justice for all those who, when caught up in conflict, were not able to have a conversation like this. And despite all those things that I have said so openly here, I would also like to think that this conversation in Ahaus is a sign of hope that theological conversation can bring us together in our common responsibility, with our different areas of competence. If this hope is justified—and how as a hope integral to our faith, could it not be?— then, one's own personal injuries aside, this conversation has to be attempted.

In the names of all of those who were able to be here, thus in my own name too, I extend heartfelt thanks to all those who have attempted this conversation, as well as to those who perhaps have not exactly found it easy to expose themselves to it. Thanks to Claudius Tanski who put our words in perspective in such a delightful manner.[1] I thank the active members of the circle of friends surrounding Johann Baptist Metz, especially Tiemo Rainer Peters, who never let himself be swayed from his idea of holding this conference. Finally, and in a particularly heartfelt way, I thank Claus Urban and all of those who have been on the ground here making this conversation possible, those who made the preparations and those whose dedicated, professional commitment provided the setting.

---

1. [Tanski played two musical interludes, one after each of the discussion periods—*trans.*]